INDEPENDENT BUSES OF SOUTH AND WEST WALES
by
Andrew Wiltshire

Eynon's of Trimsaran were very keen users of the Leyland Titan conventional front engine double-deck chassis for both service and school contract work. Even during the 1970s and early 1980s they continued to add both PD2 and PD3 models to the fleet, usually with front entrance layout and exposed radiator, and sourced them from a variety of fleets. Eynon's main route passed through Trimsaran and involved some severe hill climbing, and they soon discovered that the more modern Leyland Atlantean gave them a lot of problems, having tried four early models in 1977/8. Two slightly more unusual Leyland PD3As were purchased in 1975 from Greater Manchester PTE. UBN904/7 had East Lancs full-fronted bodywork with 73 seats and had been new to Bolton Corporation in 1962 and formed part of a batch of seventeen, eight of which had similar Metro-Cammell bodies. Also of interest and clearly visible in this view of UBN904 at Carmarthen railway station, is the large sliding entrance door. It lasted until 1980 while 907 succumbed to the breaker in 1978, but happily this unusual style of bus is represented in preservation by UBN902.

(Tony Thorne - Omnicolour)

Introduction

Having previously looked at municipal bus fleets in South Wales, we shall now turn our attention to the independent operated fleets. There were many private operators of buses throughout South and West Wales over the years. Some only traded for a few years, while others continued for decades, only to cease when there were no longer any family members to continue the business. Others eventually became victims of competition following deregulation of the bus industry in 1986, while some simply ran into, shall we say, operating difficulties. This book looks at over fifty operators who ran buses in this area during the 1960s through to the early 1980s. Only about fourteen of the fleets covered still survive in one form or another in 2009, and this clearly illustrates just how things have changed in the last twenty years or so. Since 1986 many coach operators began running buses for the first time and several new fleets appeared too. Many of these operations were short-lived and are now history, and the post-1986 events in this area really deserve a book to themselves.

What stands out when looking at independent operators is the rather individual nature of the liveries adopted by many firms and the pride taken in the appearance of their fleet, many of the vehicles being quite old but still well turned out. Sadly a few fleets struggled in this area, but then it was often the case that vehicles were used for less prestigious contract work, and only stayed in the fleet for a year or two.

Operators in this book loosely fall into three categories. Those who operated buses on stage carriage services, i.e. along a route with a timetable and for which fares were collected. Those, who in addition to stage service work, also ran buses on schools and works contracts and maybe even private hire. Finally, those who used buses only for contract or private hire work. As we are not looking at coaches in this book, I shall tend to steer clear of that side of any fleet. Initially we shall take a geographical tour of the area starting in Monmouthshire in the east and gradually moving west to the shores of Pembrokeshire and Cardiganshire.

Acknowledgements

Firstly, thank you to those who helped me with my first book and made it the success it turned out to be and to everybody who invested in a copy. Also many thanks to Bernard McCall for identifying a demand for a further book on South Wales buses, and for giving this project the green light.

As always the supply of good quality and appropriate material is fundamental to a book like this. I am very grateful to the photographers who have opened up their collections and allowed me to select the desired views. Without the work of John Jones, my father John Wiltshire and Chris Aston (Omnicolour), this project would have been a non-starter. Many thanks also to Paul Dudley, John Woodward and Richard Evans for their valued contributions and to my wife Tracey for tidying up a couple of images with her digital wizardry. My good friend John Jones has once again enthusiastically referred to his extensive library of records and notes, and from these he has been able to supply many facts and figures that have made many of the captions a lot more informative. Also, thanks to Dave B. Thomas, who has supplied details relating to the activities of Smiths of Newport, and Vernon Morgan for his clarification of services operated by West Wales Motors and Rees and Williams. Whilst being an ardent follower of many of the fleets featured, others have always remained less well-known to me, and this has meant I have learned a great deal in the preparation of this book.

Finally many thanks to my colleagues at the Wythall Transport Museum for their continued support and willingness to discuss all aspects of buses, including those unrelated to the West Midlands. Written sources used throughout include copies of Ian Allan British Bus Fleets, various editions of the Welsh Bus Handbook by Capital Transport, PSV Circle fleet histories and my own notes.

Andrew Wiltshire   Cardiff   July 2009

Published by Bernard McCall, 400 Nore Road, Portishead, Bristol, BS20 8EZ, England. Website : www.coastalshipping.co.uk
Telephone/fax : 01275 846178. E-mail : bernard@coastalshipping.co.uk
All distribution enquiries should be addressed to the publisher.

Printed by Amadeus Press, Ezra House, West 26 Business Park, Cleckheaton, West Yorkshire, BD19 4TQ
Telephone : 01274 863210; fax : 01274 863211; e-mail : info@amadeuspress.co.uk; website : www.amadeuspress.co.uk

ISBN : 978-1-902953-43-4

Front cover : Brewers of Caerau purchased an early Weymann-bodied Leyland Tiger Cub in 1954 registered OTG600, but it was not until 1966 that two similar second-hand examples were acquired from Western Welsh. A new 36 foot Leyland Leopard bus arrived in 1963, but otherwise the AEC Reliance was to remain the favoured chassis from the 1950s to the 1970s. However in 1969 a second new Tiger Cub with a Willowbrook bus body was purchased. Registered WTX334H, this bus was notable in being one of the last Tiger Cubs produced for the home market. It entered service two months after an AEC Reliance service bus, WNY453H, and was to be the last new Leyland bus purchased by Brewers, although several new Leopard coaches subsequently entered the fleet. WTX334H originally had 45 dual-purpose seats, but was refitted with 45 bus seats in 1975. The bus survived until the end, when Brewers sold the business in 1988, and is seen at Caerau on 13 February 1982. It is thought that it was subsequently preserved for a period of time.

(Paul Dudley)

Back cover : Since the late 1950s Llynfi had kept a fleet of about four double-deckers, but this changed in 1976 when they purchased four Leyland Atlanteans that had just been taken out of service by Greater Glasgow PTE. They were AGA112/26/8/9B and were given fleet numbers 133 to 136. They were well used buses, but scrubbed up nicely, and the application of Llynfi's livery to their Alexander bodies produced a pleasing result. The Atlanteans must have made an impression as a fifth example arrived the following year (CYS570B), followed by a further five from Newport Transport, between 1981 and 1984. On 1 June 1982 Atlantean 135 (AGA128B) makes its way up Neath Road, Maesteg, with the town centre in the distance. By the time the bus reached the summit, there would be an aroma of very warm oil emanating from the engine compartment. A complete lack of destination display does not help us determine where this bus is going, but the presence of male and female adults on the top deck suggests a service working to Port Talbot or Aberafan Beach rather than a steelworks service. This bus was still in use in 1984, but had left the fleet the next year.

(John Jones)

Arthur Henley did not start his career as an operator of buses, instead he ran a bakery until 1948. He closed this business in Abertillery and went on to use the premises as a bus garage. He obtained a licence to operate a stage service in late 1950 which ran to the new Roseheyworth housing estate from the town. Abertillery is a small town in the Ebbw Fach Valley which runs roughly northwards from Aberbeeg to Brynmawr, the district being known today as Blaenau Gwent. Throughout the 1950s, a variety of buses and coaches were operated, but following the acquisition of an AEC Regal from Thames Valley in 1960, the business then standardised almost exclusively on AEC Regals and later Reliances for almost twenty years. The vehicle seen here in Abertillery adjacent to the garage is *DPT308G*, a 1969-built Reliance with Plaxton Derwent 47 seat bodywork. It is at work on the Brynithel - Abertillery - Cwmtillery circular route taken over from the neighbouring Colliers' business in late 1972. This bus joined the fleet in March 1973, having been bought new by Armstrong of Ebchester in County Durham. This fine looking vehicle served the Henley fleet for an impressive thirteen years before being cannibalised in 1986.

(Tony Thorne - Omnicolour)

The Edmunds family business can be traced back to 1927 when a service from Rassau, just outside Ebbw Vale, to Markham Colliery commenced by one of the Edmunds' sons. Later his father was successful in obtaining a licence to operate a local service in 1930, which in 1931 was changed to a route which competed with Red and White. Despite objections, this service survived, albeit somewhat revised as time passed. The business became Edmunds Bus Services in 1948 and operated some very interesting buses including many double-deckers over the years. In July 1981 Edmunds experienced a vehicle crisis which led to the hire of two Leyland Leopards *FHB172/3G* from Merthyr Tydfil Borough Council and both were later purchased. Seen at Newtown, Ebbw Vale on 19 July 1982 is *FHB173G*, a 1969 bus with East Lancs bodywork. It was withdrawn in January 1983 following an accident, whereas *FHB172G* lasted with Edmunds until 1986. In 1987 the service still ran from Rassau to Briery Hill / Newtown via Carmeltown and Ebbw Vale (Palace). Edmunds surrendered the service in August 1989 to National Welsh and finally withdrew from the business of running buses and coaches in 1994. In later years, service buses included a small fleet of Bristol REs and a handful of ex-Scottish Leopards with Alexander bodies.

(John Jones)

Hills of Tredegar was one of the larger private operators on the South Wales bus scene and was particularly renowned for its impressive coach fleet which, by the mid 1970s, was one of the largest and most modern in the area. The service bus fleet was much smaller and deployed on routes around the Tredegar area, having been built up over the years by the acquisition of smaller businesses. Buses, which apart from two double deckers acquired purely for contract work, were all saloons, and were usually bought new. However in 1980, a shortage of vehicles prompted the purchase of this Metro-Cammell-bodied Leyland Leopard *JRC255D* from Middleton of Rugeley, which dated from 1966. It was a 51-seat dual-purpose vehicle that had of course started life with Trent Motor Services. As a Leopard it dovetailed nicely into the Hills fleet and here we see it in winter sunshine in Tredegar, seven years later on 21 February 1987. The bus was withdrawn in July 1990 and scrapped the following year.

(John Jones)

OUH490 was a relatively rare Leyland Olympian with Weymann bodywork with 41 seats. The 1950s Olympian was an integral version of the Tiger Cub assembled by Weymann with Leyland running units. It was new to Western Welsh, one of a batch of six similar vehicles received in 1958 with dual-purpose seating, that had followed forty bus seated Olympians into the same fleet in 1956. The bus is operating for Peake of Pontypool, who over the years had been a keen user of redundant Western Welsh buses. It is seen at Pontnewynydd on 27 October 1974, parked outside the firm's office and next to one of their two garages. *OUH490* had in fact arrived from nearby Matthews of New Inn in May 1972 and went on to serve Peake for just one further month after this photograph was taken. The origins of this operator are believed to go back as far as 1914 when a Daracq car was operated and since WWII, a fascinating collection of saloons has been owned. These include AEC Regals, a Dennis Lancet, a former Western Welsh Crossley (*DKG914*), two Beadle-AECs of Maidstone and District origin, and no fewer than eleven Tiger Cubs, to name just a few.

(John Jones)

Alan Barrington Smith commenced a coach operation from Newport, Monmouthshire, in 1968. In March 1970 he began operating service 61, Newport - Bishton - Magor jointly with Red and White, and later went on to gain sole operation of this in 1973, which he ran until 1987. In June 1970 he then took over operation of service 59, Newport-St.Brides-Cardiff. This was previously run by Davies and Baldwin of St. Brides, using minibuses, and before that by Red and White until March 1970. This 1953 Bristol LS5G, *LTA987*, was his first bus and is seen in Cardiff Bus Station on 27 July 1972, about to set off for Newport on service 59. The bus came from Western National (*1690*) in July 1970 and was sold to Martin, Weaverham for use in their contract fleet in October 1972.

Service 59 survived in this form until the November 1972, when Smiths acquired service 31, Newport-Castleton-Marshfield circular from Newport Corporation, and into this incorporated the 59, dropping the Peterstone and Cardiff section. In the spring and summer of 1972 a pair of grant specification Bedford YRQ coaches were purchased, one with Duple Viceroy Express bodywork (*XDW741K*), the other a Willowbrook Expressway (*ADW178K*), which brought much more modern and possibly more reliable vehicles to the fleet literally overnight. Smith was to surrender this service to Newport Transport on 1 July 1974, and the two Bedford coaches were also part of the deal.

(John Wiltshire)

6

This splendid looking Bristol KS5G originated with Western National as their *1828*. It had a low-bridge ECW body with seating for 55 and was new in 1950. Prance Coaches of Cardiff acquired it in July 1971 for use on the former Cardiff Corporation service 32 from Cardiff to Hensol Castle via St. Fagans. The bus is seen returning to Cardiff close to the village of Hensol on a summer day in 1971, the driver having kindly posed the bus for the photographer who was also a passenger. Despite making a superb job of repainting *LTA938* into fleet colours and even giving it fleet number *938*, this operation was short lived and the bus was sold for scrap in May 1972. Prance commenced operations in 1959 as essentially a small private hire company based in Cardiff, and over the years had numerous different bases in the city and ran many interesting second-hand coaches and a handful of buses. Of note was a new Willowbrook-bodied Ford service bus *XKG762K* acquired in January 1972 for the 32 and another short-lived Prance operation, the 33 to Morganstown.

(John Woodward)

The Pontypridd to Beddau route was served by a number of operators and in 1925 some of the smaller fleets got together to form the Amalgamated Bus Services (ABS) that was run like a cooperative. Bebb was one such member, and by the early 1950s had, in addition, started to develop a coach business. Gradually most ABS fleets sold out, and in 1969 the last two, Edwards and Maisey sold their bus interests to Bebb, to enable them to continue on their own purely as coach operators. The AEC Reliance seen here in Pontypridd on 22 May 1975 in Bebb livery is quite an interesting vehicle. *652GVA* was new to Scottish operator Irvine of Salsburgh in August 1963 and it had a Plaxton Highway 55 seat body. By 1967 it was working for MacGregor of Sible Hedingham in Essex as their *L53* and, in a surprise move, passed into the Colchester Corporation fleet as their number *55* in June 1970. Bebb acquired the bus in April 1973 and gave it fleet their number *31*. It was to be a regular performer on the Pontypridd to Beddau service until 1978 when it was sold to Kenfig Motors of Kenfig Hill where it lasted a further twelve months before being broken up. Bebb continued trading until 2006 when they sold out to the French-owned Veolia group. By this time they had quite an impressive portfolio of bus services throughout South-East Wales, as well as being a major player on the National Express network.

(John Jones)

The R I Davies business from Tredegar originated in 1927 and operated mainly Leylands from the late 1930s until the early 1960s. The founder died in 1961 and the business continued to be run and expanded by his son Hilling Davies. Double-deckers appeared in 1965 following the acquisition of Wheatsheaf of Merthyr which brought with it two services. *NDR87* was one of a pair of former Plymouth Corporation Leyland PD2s added to the fleet in October 1973. It dates from 1957 has a Metro-Cammell 56-seat body and is seen about to join the ring road in Merthyr and head off to Trefechan on 3 July 1974. Prior to this, the service buses had tended to be turned out in either a grey and red or green and cream livery, and *NDR87* marked a change to grey with dark blue bands, while *NDR90* had an overall advertisement livery for a Sony TV dealership. Both the PD2s were taken out of service and sold in February 1975. The more glamorous side of the business was that of continental coach holidays, which saw the purchase of many high specification luxury coaches during the early 1970s, including some of the first Volvos. With the sudden death of Hilling Davies in February 1975, the company had lost its guiding light, and in September of 1976 the business passed to Hills of Tredegar, the bus services having already having been acquired by Merthyr Tydfil Borough Council in March 1976.

(John Wiltshire)

During World War II a Mr T M (Tommy) Morris from Pencoed took over the private hire and works services from a family member. The business developed and by 1972 two small firms, John Hemmings of Llanharran and Pioneer Motors of Kenfig Hill, were acquired. At this stage, works services and private hire were the core activities and the name Morris Travel Ltd was established in 1973. Although four former Birmingham Corporation Daimler COG5s were operated in the period 1949-52, the next double-deckers did not arrive until 1974, and these unusual acquisitions came from the same part of the country. Purchased from Midland Red were six BMMO D9s *2965/72/76/93, 3017, 6336HA*, all with 72-seat rear entrance bodies and platform doors. *2993HA* was used for spares but the others entered service in Morris Travel blue. The D9 was a technically advanced integral vehicle with semi-automatic transmission, hydraulic brakes, rubber suspension and disc brakes on the front wheels. *2972HA* is seen here at Morris's Wellhouse garage in Pencoed on 3 July 1975, reversing into its off-road parking space after completing a school run that morning. Just as unusual was the purchase of a trio of BMMO S16 saloons at the same time, followed for a few months only, in 1975, by a pair of BMMO CM6T coaches. Morris usually ran their buses for a maximum of two years and the Midland Red buses were replaced in 1976 by eight rather more conventional ex-Glasgow Leyland Atlanteans.

(John Wiltshire)

As one of the popular Welsh surnames, there were inevitably a number of operators named Thomas working in South and West Wales. One such operation was Thomas Coaches which was based in the Rhondda area and in particular could be seen around Tonypandy and Penygraig. The business began in 1967 and from 1978 the vehicles were parked up at the Welcome Inn car park in Clydach Vale. New coaches started to arrive from 1972 and this side of the business continued to develop. The first double-deckers arrived in 1978 in the form of two ex-Brighton Leyland PD2s. These were followed by three rare Albion Lowlanders, all LR1 models with pneumocyclic transmission, one of which was used for spares only. One of a pair from Highland Omnibuses was *UCS628* which is seen at Porthcawl on a private hire turn on 15 July 1979. This view clearly shows how the Alexander body seems to accentuate the high driving position, something other bodybuilders on this chassis successfully disguised. New to Western SMT in 1963, it lasted with Thomas for only around eighteen months. Further double-deckers took the form of more PD2s as well as Bristol FLFs. Several Leyland Atlanteans appeared from 1981 followed by Leyland Fleetlines and Bristol VRTs by the late 1980s. Thomas Coaches still trades today, but based in part of the former Rhondda Transport and National Welsh garage at Porth.

(John Jones)

Llynfi Motor Services was a smart and well-respected operator based at Maesteg, a large mining community in the Llynfi Valley to the north of Bridgend. It was founded around 1921 by William Thomas, a local miner. His first vehicle, a Fiat was reputedly worked between Maesteg and Caerau for a short time in that year. We know for certain that the route to Port Talbot was started in 1923, using a newly built road over the mountain from Maesteg. This route which was operated right up to the end of Llynfi in 1988, was periodically shared with South Wales Transport and later extended to Aberafan Beach. Upon the death of its founder, the business passed to Martha Thomas in 1937, one of several female bus operators in the area at this time. Double-deckers first appeared in 1957 but were always in the minority. In 1971 a pair of fine-looking AEC Regent Vs with front-entrance Willowbrook bodies arrived from South Wales Transport. Numbered *111* and *112* (*VWN956/7*) they had been re-numbered to *107* and *108* by 19 May 1975, when we see *108* parked up at the depot. Both these buses left the fleet in 1982. *VWN 956* went for scrap, but the subject of this photograph was exported to Italy and is believed to exist still in the warmer climes of southern Europe.

(John Wiltshire)

The other major independent operator to serve the town of Maesteg was A E & F R Brewer from Caerau at the head of the Llynfi valley. These brothers were dairy farmers who ran their first bus in 1921 on a service from Caerau to the Maesteg area. In the 1930s they were running into Maesteg town centre with two routes, and, as the area developed with new housing, further services were launched to areas such as Llangynwyd, Cwmfelin and Turberville. Other work included schools and works contracts and excursions, and private hire became a substantial part of the business using a fleet of coaches, most of which were bought new. A blue, cream and turquoise livery was used until the mid-1980s and vehicle policy was focussed on Leyland, Dennis and Bedford until 1939 when a new AEC Regal arrived. In the post-war years Bedfords continued to appear, but AEC became the principal choice for most buses and coaches. Many AEC Regals were followed by over 30 Reliances from 1954 until 1981. *278TNY* is a 1963 model with a Weymann 53-seat bus body and is seen at Porthcawl on 25 July 1976. The bus survived until 1988 when Brewers sold out to South Wales Transport subsidiary Helproute, which went on to perpetuate the Brewer fleetname.

(John Jones)

Porthcawl Omnibus Company as the name suggests hailed from the small seaside town of Porthcawl, not far from Bridgend. Prior to World War II, Porthcawl was host to a number of small operators using vehicles up to a maximum of 14 seats, but after hostilities ceased, they came together as Porthcawl Omnibus Co Ltd. Before the 1940s ended they had taken over both Pines Garages and A Shute, Porthcawl, and around 1955 took over the local services from Western Welsh. In 1959 the company was acquired by E P John (Kenfig Motors Ltd) and eventually both fleets were based at Kenfig Hill. Porthcawl town services continued to be licensed to POC with Kenfig buses regularly operating on hire. Pairs of vehicles would often be allocated one to each

company. In 1965 John Williams, a former POC driver, took over one of the town services and in 1977 he took over the company, which separated from Kenfig Motors at this point. For a time the new operation saw vehicles licensed to both Porthcawl Omnibus Co and J Williams, running two local services in Porthcawl and a Bridgend to Porthcawl service. Porthcawl Omnibus added two ex-London Transport Regents to their fleet in June 1970. These were *KGK673*, and the bus seen here at Kenfig Hill on 5 March 1975, *LYR875*. This particular bus had been *RT3456* with London Transport and had a Saunders body. Porthcawl Omnibus kept it until 1976 when it was sold to a preservationist in the Bristol area. However by 2006 its continued existence was in doubt.

(John Jones)

Jenkins of Skewen was another well-known name amongst the independent fleets to be found in South Wales and it can be traced back to the mid-1920s. Pre-war purchases included an ex-Huddersfield AEC Regal and a number of ex-South Wales Transport Dennis buses. After the war Jenkins eventually standardised on Bedford for most of its coach requirements. Works contracts at this time were to local collieries, though contracts were later obtained to serve the BP oil refinery at nearby Llandarcy, and this brought Leyland Tiger Cubs from Rhondda and Leyland Olympians and an Albion Nimbus from Western Welsh, all painted in a maroon livery. The Jenkins contract fleet by the mid-1970s had a strong Bristol flavour, but by the early 1980s they had standardised

the contract fleet on lightweight buses. Initially six Ford buses, three from Alder Valley and three from Trent were used, eventually being joined by six ECW-bodied Bristol LH6Ls also of National Bus Company origin. The Fords were interesting as two of the Alder Valley examples had ECW bodies, the third had a Plaxton body and all were Ford R1014 models. One of the former Trent trio is seen at Barry Island on a private hire duty on 26 June 1982, when the coach park at this seaside resort was regularly packed with buses and coaches. *NNN397P*, a longer wheelbase Ford R1114 model, dated from 1976 and had a Willowbrook body with seating for 49. It passed to Shearings in December 1988, when they acquired the Jenkins business.

(Paul Dudley)

13

Cream Line was from the small mining community of Tonmawr near Neath, the business being developed over the years by D T Davies and his family. Passengers were initially carried in adapted goods lorries, and a car hire firm was operated in the 1920s. They were originally known as Cream Line Services, but in the late 1970s the name Creamline as one word started to appear on some vehicles. The main service ran into Neath from Tonmawr and over the years other services from Neath to Pontrhydyfen, Penyard and the Glanant Estate were operated. The favoured chassis manufacturer had been Leyland for many years, although Bedford and Bristol LS saloons were also to be found. A new Leyland Tiger Cub, with Duple Midland body, KWN246, appeared in 1954, while from the mid-1960s many used examples appeared. Six examples obtained locally from Thomas Bros, Port Talbot, featured three of each Weymann and Saro bodies. Later Tiger Cubs included four obtained from Midland Red (Stratford Blue) including 2745AC, seen parked on the driveway into the yard at Tonmawr on 19 May 1975. It dates from 1959 and has a Willowbrook body.

(John Wiltshire)

Ken Hopkins was based at Tonna in the Neath valley, having started out in the 1950s running a small fleet of coaches. His first bus arrived in 1968 in the form of a Leyland Tiger Cub from Western Welsh. The subject of this photograph is MOD970, a 1952 Bristol LS5G, which Hopkins purchased in 1972 from Western National, and is seen in the yard at Tonna looking a little faded on 29 April 1973. Obviously impressed with his Bristol LS, a further six examples followed, one of which was a coach from Crosville, and another, MAX118, had come from Alder Valley but was new to Red and White. In 1976 two Bristol MWs appeared from Bristol Omnibus, but the fleet was always primarily a coaching concern. However, a few double-deckers did appear in 1999/2000 but were relatively short-lived, and a brand new Transbus Enviro 300 saloon arrived in 2005, painted yellow, for use as a school bus. It is pleasing to record that the Ken Hopkins fleet still trades in 2009.

(John Jones)

Morris Bros of Swansea started out in 1951 as a small coach operation and expanded throughout the 1950s and 1960s latterly acquiring several smaller operators in the locality. Also acquired along the way was a road haulage business, and the family also diversified into van and lorry hire. Morris Bros of Swansea became a limited company in 1973 by which time it was operating a large fleet of smartly turned-out buses on contract work as well as a mixed bag of coaches. By 1976 the double deck fleet was even bigger and more varied, and included a number of AEC Regent Vs. This example, *758NDT*, was a particularly interesting vehicle, and is seen at the depot on 25 June 1976. It was purchased in 1975 from Blue Ensign of Doncaster by whom it had been bought new in 1964. Morris had a contract to serve the B&I ferry terminal at Swansea for a service to Eire, and *758NDT* carries a number of notices in its windows advertising this. This bus had obviously been well looked after and continued to serve Morris Bros until May 1984, when this fine fleet sold out to Cleverly of Cwmbran. A year later *758NDT* was sold for preservation to a Mr Hurst of Doncaster, but a body defect in the roof saw it being converted to open-top, and later exported to Germany, where it now resides in a transport museum.

(John Wiltshire)

Morriston, in the lower Swansea valley, was home to Bryn Davies Coaches, a small coach firm started in 1949 by Brynmor Davies with a Bedford OB coach. By 1966, the business was being run by his son Daryl Davies, and he used the D Coaches fleetname which first appeared in 1969. This was followed by the acquisition of several small neighbouring operators, and the business was set to expand very rapidly in the early 1970s. A Dennis bus was owned briefly in 1951/2 , the next bus being an ex-Western Welsh Albion Nimbus *TUH22* bought and sold in 1971. Shortly after this, some new

contract work witnessed the arrival of a number of Bristols in the form of Lodekkas and LS saloons and also this Leyland PD2, *LFS423*, from Cream Line of Tonmawr (see page 36). This bus is looking very smart having been painted in D Coaches' simple but effective livery of light grey with an orange band. This shot was taken in the weak but dramatic winter sunshine of 21 January 1975, and parked behind the PD2 we see one of the pair of Seddon Pennine VIs with Duple 57-seat bodies, *DCY43/44K*, bought new in February 1972.

(John Wiltshire)

16

South Wales Transport made service cuts in the Ammanford area in 1971, as a result of which, a redundant driver, Peter Smith, set up in business to operate the Ammanford to Pontardulais and Ammanford to Hopkinstown services in September of that year. Initially he hired vehicles from D-Coaches of Morriston, but eventually he acquired his own fleet. This troubled operation struggled on until 1975 when a limited company, Triafon Ltd, was formed, and later Pathlin Ltd appeared in 1976. All bus operations had ceased by 1977. The vehicle seen here, *HMS241*, parked at Ammanford on 4 August 1976, was licensed to the Triafon operation. It was one of four similar AEC Reliances that started life with Scottish Bus Group fleet Alexander Northern, and dating from 1956, had an Alexander body with 45 seats. It was withdrawn shortly after this photograph was taken.

(John Jones)

John Lewis, also of Morriston, was another relatively short-lived bus operator that sprang up in business with a Ford Transit in January 1971 and had completely left the PSV business by the end of 1978. Despite this they operated some varied and interesting types of bus. Two Bristol LS6Bs of 1958 vintage arrived from United Automobile in 1971. John Lewis must have gained some extra school contracts from September 1974 as there was an influx of used buses at this time, all of which were to be repainted into the distinctive livery as seen in this view. The buses included Leyland Tiger Cubs and Bristol MW saloons together with at least half a dozen double-deckers. Two AEC Regent Vs and a pair of Bristol Lodekkas were joined by an ex Northampton Daimler CVG6 (*GVV206*) and this rather splendid and rare lowbridge Massey-bodied Guy Arab IV. *UTH78*, was acquired in 1974 from Rees and Williams, of Tycroes, to whom it had been new in January 1960, and is seen on the road adjacent to Lewis's yard in Morriston on 3 June 1975.

(John Wiltshire)

17

Clydach is a small town situated south west of Pontardawe in the lower Swansea valley and was home to R J Jones and Sons, who traded as East End Garage, and ran a small fleet of quite interesting buses and coaches, mainly on contract work. Operations began in August 1961 with a Commer minibus. In the 1970s, they operated two Dennis Lolines which were rare in South Wales. The Loline was a Bristol Lodekka that was built under licence by Dennis Motors and therefore made available to non-Tilling companies. Both of the Jones' Lolines were MkIII models, new to North Western Road Car in 1961 and had Alexander front-entrance bodies. The first to arrive was *RDB884* from SELNEC PTE in January 1974. It was joined by *RDB872* in April 1976 after a spell with Ayrshire operator Shennan of Drongan. Both would receive the light blue livery and were the first double-deckers for the East End fleet. *RDB872* is seen at Clydach on 26 November 1980, by which time sister vehicle *884* had been scrapped. Fairly prominent in this view is the illuminated advertisement panel which has been painted over at some stage in the past. *872* was fortunate as when it was deemed surplus in early 1983, it was snapped up by the Loline Preservation Group of Manchester and is believed to exist still.

(Andrew Wiltshire)

Eynon's were one of the more well-known independent fleets from South Wales possibly due to the nature of their routes and the great variety of buses, including many double-deckers, that they purchased and ran over the years. Trimsaran was a mining village situated between Llanelli and Kidwelly on what is now the B4308. Samuel Eynon and his sons originally worked at Trimsaran Colliery and purchased their first vehicle in 1917, and began operating from Llanelli to Trimsaran in 1921 or 1922 with a new Leyland, despite competition from other operators. In 1926 this route was extended to Carmarthen, and by 1930 Eynon's were running three routes in the area. In the 1960s and 1970s various services were added including the former Western Welsh service from Llanelli to Carmarthen via Pontyberem in 1971. With time, Leyland became the preferred choice for the majority of service buses and the first double-decker arrived in 1948. In 1971 Eynon's purchased five Metro-Cammell-bodied PD2s from Plymouth Corporation and ran them until 1974 when they were then replaced by a former Trent PD2 and a further four from Plymouth including *OCO514* & *519*. Two of these are seen in Trimsaran on 18 October 1975. *OCO514* was thought to be working a relief service from Kidwelly to Llanelli while further down the street *519* was the main service bus from Carmarthen to Llanelli. Both were withdrawn in 1976, *519* becoming a tree-lopper for Eynon's and surviving as such until 1982.

(John Jones)

The first service to be operated by West Wales Motors Ltd was from Llanelli to Ammanford which commenced in 1929. An operating base at Tycroes was established in 1931 and the same year a new route from Swansea to Llandeilo was launched. The following year saw the introduction of the well-known colour scheme of grey, cream and red, which remained largely unchanged until the end of operations. The first coaches were introduced to the fleet in 1947 and, in 1976 the failed Triafon fleet (see page 17) at Ammanford was taken over. Vehicle acquisitions have always been interesting and prewar Albions and TSM were favoured almost exclusively, including several double deckers. Wartime Guys were very favourably received leading to their virtual monopoly of new buses until an ill-fated Wulfrunian in 1960, which was sold after only 15 months use. For a half-cab, *97* (*ASC654B*) was a late addition in the West Wales fleet arriving from Eynon's of Trimsaran in June 1983 at a time when West Wales had already acquired a taste for the Atlantean. It is a Leyland PD3/6 with a front entrance Alexander body that started life with Edinburgh Corporation Transport in 1964. It is seen waiting on the garage forecourt at Tycroes on 2 July 1983 having been freshly painted in West Wales colours. Surprisingly it lasted for only two months.

(John Jones)

Also hailing from the village of Tycroes was Rees and Williams, an operation started by the Rees family around 1920. By 1923, and trading as Rees and Williams, they were running a service from Ammanford to Pontardulais, and by 1926 were to be found running into Llanelli and then by 1927 to Llandeilo. Subsequent developments were complex but needless to say West Wales Motors commenced in Tycroes in 1931 by a Rees and Williams director. West Wales adopted Rees and Williams livery, so a maroon, red and cream livery was adopted, and for a time, the Tycroes and District fleetname was used. As might be expected, relations between the two operations were strained for many years. The year 1966 witnessed the arrival of two new saloons for Rees and Williams. A lightweight Ford R192 with Strachans bodywork was joined by *FBX474D*, a far more business-like Leyland Tiger Cub with 44-seat body by Marshall. It is seen heading through Tycroes on 28 July 1973, bound for Swansea on the service from Llandeilo, and about to pass its owner's garage, just out of sight to the left of the picture. As a matter of interest, the West Wales garage was on the right hand side, at the bottom of the hill behind the bus. *FBX474D* was to be sold in 1978 to Thomas of Llangadog, another smart fleet.

(John Jones)

W J Davies came from the village of Pencader located approximately ten miles to the north of Carmarthen. The family originally ran a public house and, after running several taxis, moved into bus operations in 1926. D S Davies joined his brother in 1930, and Davies Brothers, Blossom Garage, Pencader was formed. However, in 1948 D S Davies left to form his own haulage and coach company. At the 1930 Road Traffic Act, Davies Bros was running Carmarthen to Lampeter, Carmarthen to Llandysul and Lampeter. J D Davies succeeded his father in 1970 following which the business expanded raidly. The fleet of Dan Jones of Abergwili near Carmarthen was acquired in 1978 and with it came Carmarthen town services, the Llandeilo to Carmarthen route, and a depot.

Davies Bros tended to buy most saloons from new and Leyland Leopards were followed by Bristol LHs and Bedfords. An ECW-bodied LH6L, *HBX948N*, was followed by *98* (*KBX38P*), a much more unusual example with Duple Dominant 53-seat body featuring 3+2 seating towards the rear. It was new in 1975 and is seen here at Carmarthen railway station claiming to be heading off to Llandysul at some point. Only four Duple Dominant bus bodies were built on Bristol LH chassis, two of these going to the nearby fleet of Silcox at Pembroke Dock. *KBX38P* was sold in October 1985 to Nuttall of Modbury in South Devon.

(Tony Thorne - Omnicolour)

Another small West Wales fleet to have its roots in the 1920s was Jones Motors from Login, a small village about five miles north west of Whitland. A certain Mr D C Thomas of Ffailwen started out with a Ford bus before going into the road haulage business. During World War II one of his lorries was converted to carry passengers and in 1945, together with a Mr Idwal Jones, formed a company titled Thomas and Jones (Clynderwen) Ltd, which became Precelly Motors Ltd in 1948 and operated rural routes in the area. Idwal Jones' son Arwel started up as Jones of Login in 1965 with his late father's share of Precelly Motors, acquiring the reminder on Mr Thomas' retirement in 1972. In 1981 the vehicles and the Pendine to Carmarthen route of Pioneer, Laugharne, the successor to the well-known Tudor Williams "Pioneer" operation, were purchased. An interesting Bedford from the 1950s is seen at the Login depot on 2 June 1976, one of the vehicles acquired from Precelly Motors in 1972. *RTX497* was an SBO model with a Duple Midland bus body seating 40, and was new to Williams of Treorchy in the Rhondda in July 1955. It was withdrawn in 1974, and became derelict at the depot by April 1977. Jones of Login operates a modern, immaculate fleet in 2009.

(John Jones)

Tudor Williams of Laugharne who traded as Pioneer Services commenced operation in 1908 with a horse bus service between Laugharne and St. Clears. Motor buses appeared in 1914, and in 1937, the first of many Dennis Lancets entered service. Double-deckers appeared in 1946 and eventually included Leylands, AECs, Guy Arabs, a Dennis Lance, an Albion Venturer and a Daimler CWA6; quite a variety. Laugharne is a small town in Carmarthenshire, south of St Clears and situated on the estuary of the River Taf. With the passing of Pioneer's operations, one of the remaining attractions has to be the castle, which was eventually left to fall to ruin in the 18th century. Reflecting happier times in the town, which was home to the poet Dylan Thomas, are these three buses from the Pioneer fleet lined up in their owners yard in Laugharne in June 1973. From left to right we have *FMO16*, a 1950 Bristol L6B with ECW 35 seat body new to Thames Valley, *PMW386* a former Silver Star Leyland Tiger Cub with unusual Harrington bodywork that was latterly with Wilts and Dorset, and lastly *UTX9*, a former Caerphilly UDC Massey-bodied Leyland Royal Tiger of 1957. *PMW386* was the last of this trio to run in service, remaining until around August 1975.

Chris Aston (Omnicolour)

The Silcox family was active in business in Pembroke Dock as early as 1882, and entered the bus business in 1923, by taking over the Pembroke and Tenby services of John Ford of Pembroke. The present garage and works at Waterloo was built in 1939 and the World War II brought much business from the naval dockyard at nearby Pembroke dock and saw the fleet double in size to around two dozen vehicles. The coming of the oil industry to the area in the early 1960s boosted business further and the opening of the Cleddau Bridge in March 1975 allowed Silcox to expand operations into the towns of Neyland, Milford and Haverfordwest. By the 1970s, Silcox had obtained a substantial number of contracts over a large area and for a while out-stationed some of its buses at Neyland and Tenby. Although the heyday of the double-decker at Silcox was over by this time, they still kept a relatively small number for school duties, and *804SHW* was one of three Bristol FLFs purchased in 1978 from Bristol Omnibus. It is seen here in a lay-by near Johnston on 18 March 1987, parked up for the day in between school runs and with other Silcox buses for company. After several Bristol FLFs, Silcox turned to the Bristol VRT for its double-deck requirements. As for *804SHW* it was later re-registered *ADE146A*, and when sold passed to Top Deck Travel for use as a mobile caravan for touring Europe and places farther afield. It was last heard of in 1996.

(Andrew Wiltshire)

In 2009 West Wales based Richards Bros is one of the largest independent operators in the principality, but its history only goes back as far as 1939. This is when W G Richards started a haulage company in connection with RNAD military base at Trecwn near Fishguard. The carriage of people in vans was superseded when the first bus was purchased in 1943. In the post-war years, school contracts developed and a coach business was established. W G Richards obtained its first services in 1958 when it took over Williams of Cardigan. This now gave it two bases, one at Moylgrove and a new one in Cardigan, and a further service from St Davids to Fishguard was obtained from Western Welsh in 1970/1. In 1972 they took over the services of Williams of St Dogmaels,

and in 1976, Roberts (Pioneer) of Newport, which had been operating three former Western Welsh services of significance. In 1981 the service from St Davids to Haverfordwest, previously operated by Marchwood Motorways, was acquired. Bedford buses and coaches have dominated the fleet from the start and a few still remain on fleet strength in 2009. *FDE782L* was a very typical Bedford SB5 that was acquired with the Roberts of Newport business in 1976. The bus, which has Willowbrook bodywork, was new in 1972, and it is seen at Fishguard on 12 April 1982.

(John Jones)

We shall now take a look at some ex-BET group Tiger Cubs. British Electric Traction group fleets began to dispose of their early Leyland Tiger Cubs in the mid-1960s, and these proved to be very attractive vehicles for the many small privately owned fleets around the UK. They were reliable and economical buses and offered the possibility for one man operation. Llynfi purchased their first Tiger Cub way back in 1955, when they were able to acquire the well-travelled Saro-bodied Leyland demonstrator *OTC738*, which went on to serve Llynfi for around twenty years. The next Tiger Cub buses arrived in 1966/7 and included a Weymann-bodied pair from Thomas Bros of Port Talbot (*NNY56/60*). There followed two from Trent (*FCH11/16*) and one from East Midland (*ORR325*) all with Saro bodies. Further Weymann examples were of Western Welsh origin together with *FCH23* which was new to Trent but arrived from Davies of Pencader in 1969. *FCH23* looks very well cared for in this view taken on 19 May 1975 in the depot yard. Note the unusual Leyland badge on the front of the bus, added by George Thomas, a practice he followed for many years. The vehicle was then an impressive 21 years old and would shortly be sold for further service to an operator in the Morriston area.

(John Wiltshire)

Seen in Laugharne on 16 April 1974 is *OUP662*, a 1954 Tiger Cub with a lightweight 44-seat Saunders-Roe body. It was new to Sunderland District Omnibus Company and was one of a batch of thirteen similar buses. It is owned by Pioneer (Tudor Williams) of Laugharne and was purchased from Thomas of Llangadog in March 1971, and ran until 1974. It is quite apparent that Leyland Tiger Cubs were a very popular choice for Carmarthenshire operators in the 1960s and 1970s. Saunders-Roe was based at Beaumaris on Anglesey, and built nearly 150 Saro aluminium bodies on quite a number of early Tiger Cubs for BET group customers such as Ribble, East Midland, Thomas Bros, Yorkshire Traction and Trent. The main distinguishing feature of this attractive body was deep decorative trim around the bus at wheel-arch level. Until 1971 Pioneer operated Carmarthen to Pendine via St Clears and Laugharne jointly with Western Welsh, when they closed their depot in Carmarthen and the Laugharne outstation, and pulled out of this arrangement. Originally they had taken over their portion of this service from Ebsworth of Laugharne in December 1954.

(John Jones)

The livery of grey and white used by Peake of Pontypool did little to enhance the appearance of its vehicles, and former Stratford Blue Leyland Tiger Cub *5452WD* seems to be no exception. This bus was originally one of a batch of five delivered to Stratford Blue in 1962 with Marshall bodywork and dual-purpose seating for 41 passengers and came to Peakes alongwith *5449WD* in April 1973 having previously worked for Williams and Davies of Wrexham. It is seen in Pontypool on 6 April 1974, but gives us little idea of its destination. We do know that, at the start of the decade, Peake ran five local bus services from Pontypool, to exotic destinations such as Pantygasseg, Abersychan, Trevethin and Waunddu. They were still operating in the 1980s when the choice of vehicle had switched to Leyland Leopards and later Bristol REs. Just prior to deregulation in 1986 three former London Transport DMS type Fleetlines were placed into service, the first double-deckers to be operated since a former South Wales Transport Leyland TD5, *BCY578*, was withdrawn from use in 1960. Ian Peake ceased to operate bus services, going out of business in February 1987, but later re-entered the industry as a purely coaching concern.

(John Wiltshire)

Western Welsh was the largest customer for the Leyland Tiger Cub in the United Kingdom taking a total of 349 examples. The first of these arrived in October 1953 and they were still receiving new Tiger Cubs until December 1967, three years after the first examples had been withdrawn and sold. *MUH180* was a 1957 delivery having a Weymann Hermes body with seating for 44. It is seen here on 5 March 1975 with Nelsons Coaches of Glyn Neath who acquired it in January 1971 and gave it fleet number *1*. The paint job appears to be fairly recent but the bus does seem to have acquired a few nasty dents. This operator started out in 1949 at Glyn Neath as Nelson and Richards, but by 1959 was trading solely as Nelson's. At this time they operated just four coaches, all Commers, and in 1967 a new Ford was purchased. *MUH180* was Nelson's first bus and lasted until 1979 when it went for scrap, to be replaced by an ex-Ribble Leyland Leopard. A second similar Leopard arrived shortly after this, and in 1991 a coach-seated Leyland National of London Transport origin joined the fleet. This added a little variety to what has always been regarded as a well respected coach fleet in the area.

(John Jones)

Porthcawl Omnibus bought a pair of distinctive, if not a little heavy-looking Leyland Tiger Cubs from Yorkshire Traction in May 1972 primarily for use on Porthcawl services. NHE114/115 had been new in 1958 and were part of a batch of 23 similar buses, the only Park Royal-bodied saloons ever purchased by Yorkshire Traction. Back in South Wales we see NHE115 parked opposite the Grand Pavilion on Porthcawl Esplanade on a rather damp and dreary 3 August 1973. The clock behind says 12.14 if we believe it, but there are no holiday makers in sight. Regardless of this, the bus will no doubt make the trip to Trecco Bay, home to one of the largest caravan parks in Europe. The style of body is enhanced by the alloy trim at headlamp level, and the application of black to the window surrounds sets the livery off well. Although clearly displaying Porthcawl Omnibus fleetnames, documentation tells us that NHE115 had by now been transferred to the associated Kenfig Motors operation with whom it worked until April 1975. NHE114 on the other hand remained with POC, and survived until November 1977. Some interesting double-deckers operated by POC and associated Kenfig Motors included Stratford Blue Leyland PD2s, Guy Arab IVs from Northern General and Edinburgh Corporation and a very interesting AEC/Hanson rebuild (VVH348) with Roe double-deck bodywork.

(John Wiltshire collection)

D Jones and Son, of Abergwili near Carmarthen, was a very old established firm which began way back in the 1890s with horse transport, but was operating a motor vehicle by 1905. After World War I there were routes from Carmarthen and Llandeilo, and possibly to Lampeter, and by the 1930s destinations such as Llanelli and Ammanford were served. Dan Jones as the firm became known locally, took full advantage of the decision in 1971 by Western Welsh to withdraw from Carmarthen and close its depot in the town, by taking over the town services and for a short while ran the service to Llanybri. Jones was a keen Leyland user and took a number of used Tiger Cubs, but other buses operated prior to 1970 included such gems as Daimler CVD6 in double and single-deck form, a pair of early Albion Nimbus and two Leyland PD2s, one coming from Ribble, the other being a former James of Ammanford bus. This former North Western Tiger Cub *KDB690* was given fleet number *14*, and was one of a pair purchased by Jones in May 1971. It dated from 1957 and had a Weymann body. North Western was a keen Tiger Cub user, and a number of examples subsequently found their way to South Wales. By the time this photo was taken at the depot on 24 October 1973, it had been withdrawn from service, despite looking to be in very good order externally. It may have been retained for possible reinstatement as it was still owned in October 1974. A similar bus to this, *KBD696*, has been saved for preservation.

(John Jones)

29

Now we look at some "classic" bus designs. It is sometimes difficult and controversial to define what should be regarded as a "classic bus"; it is often a matter of personal choice. Few however could argue that the Bedford OB was anything but a classic. The village of Maenclochog north of Narbeth in Pembrokeshire was home to two operators in the mid-1950s, O J Edwards and T C Herbert, with Edwards being a relative newcomer to bus operation. Both fleets were largely made up of Bedfords fitted with bus bodies, and Herbert sold out to Edwards in March 1960. Between 1963 and 1965 Edwards purchased four Bedford OBs with Duple bus bodies from the Ministry of Supply with registrations *JXW461/87* and *JXW858/72*, and, as no stage services were operated, these would be used for many years on contract work to the RNAD depot at Trecwn. In September 1973 a new operator, T L Jenkins, took over the Edwards business and by 1974 had formed a limited company Eltys Motors Ltd. *JXW872* is seen near the church at Maenclochog on 16 April 1974 covered in country road grime. It was withdrawn by the following August and had became derelict by April 1977. The last of these Bedfords were withdrawn by 1980, but went on to survive in the undergrowth near the disused railway station for many years. In 2009 a Mr E J Lewis who was associated with T L Jenkins still operates six vehicles from Maenclochog.

(John Jones)

The first double-decker for Eynon's, as already mentioned, arrived in 1948 and was a Leyland Titan TD2 from Red and White. This was followed by a pair of new Leyland-bodied PD2s, *FTH831* in 1950 and *GBX987* in 1951. The first of ten ex-London Transport RTLs would arrive in 1958, the last being purchased in 1965. This interesting view at the Trimsaran garage on 17 August 1970 depicts *LYF35* and *LYF40* which joined the Eynon's fleet in 1963. In their London days they carried fleet numbers *RTL1111/6*. The RTL was a 7ft 6in wide Leyland PD2 that was heavily modified to be interchangeable with RT bodies and had London Transport's standard transmission; these two examples dated from 1951 and had Park Royal bodies. Both buses seem to be well decked out with advertisements for local businesses and proudly display their owner's name all around the bus. The RTLs served Eynon's well and the last examples survived until August 1971. In 1970 Eynon's then took four conventional RT type AEC Regents from London Transport, but these had all gone by the end of 1972.

(John Jones)

The class of Leyland PD3 double-decker with full-fronted Northern Counties front-entrance bodies purchased by Southdown Motor Services between 1957 and 1967 became known as the "Queen Mary" and was arguably one of the classic double-deck designs of the twentieth century. Three of the 285 former Southdown examples found their way into the fleets of South Wales independents. Morris Bros had *XUF851* and Cream Line obtained similar *XUF844* in August 1973 from the Sussex fleet where it had been number *844*. The bus, which dated from 1959 and had seating for 69, is seen here in Neath bus station on a murky 29 August 1974. The destination blind tells us that it is due to leave for Tonmawr via Cimla, and it is worth noting that both double-deckers and saloons were used on this service. Following a break of over ten years, double-deckers reappeared in 1967 when the Leyland Titan was the preferred type, although a trio of Bristol Lodekkas from Crosville Motor Services, and two early Atlanteans of Newcastle Corporation origin were later tried. *XUF844* was withdrawn in 1978 and sold to a breaker in the Bridgend area.

(John Wiltshire)

The Bristol LS was introduced in 1951, being an under-floor engine single-deck bus for the benefit of the Tilling group fleets and its sale thus restricted to these fleets alone. Most had five or six cylinder engines by Gardner or a six cylinder Bristol engine, and all had bodywork by ECW. Silcox had for many years been a keen user of Bristol chassis having purchased a number of K and L models before restrictions prevented any more being acquired. However by 1970 some early Bristol LS saloons were appearing on the second-hand market and Silcox acquired almost thirty of them including OTT50 and 63 acquired from Western National in 1970. Three years later they were joined by OTT49/52/56/59 that had been in use with Cream Line of Tonmawr for a while. OTT49 acquired the Silcox fleet number 121 and went on to give a further four years service in Pembrokeshire. It ended its days as a non-PSV in the Pembroke Dock area by the end of the decade. In happier times we see OTT49 at Tenby on 20 April 1976, hiding its age well and still looking every inch a classic bus of the 1950s.

(John Jones)

Right : In addition to the Bristol LS saloon (see page 6), A B Smith of Newport went on to purchase a Bristol KSW6B from Western National (*1850*) in May 1971. *LTA993* was actually new to Southern National in 1952 and had a lowbridge ECW body with seating for 55. The bus was still carrying its original Tilling green and cream livery when seen here in Dock Street, Newport, on 22 July 1972, making an appearance on the Cardiff service 59 which ran via St Brides and Peterstone. Behind *LTA993* is a Newport Corporation Leyland Atlantean adjacent to the old bus pull-in, and the large building in the background with the tower structure houses Newport's indoor market, which is still very much in evidence in 2009. *LTA993* was to be taken out of service in the September of that year and was sold to Martins, the Middlewich dealer the following month. By this time the title of the firm had changed to Smith's of Newport Ltd, and the next double-decker to arrive would be a former Cumberland Motor Services Bristol Lodekka, *XAO608*. In the 1970s Smith operated two contract services for workers at clothing manufacturer H Lotery Ltd, from Bettws Estate and also Ringland Estate to its site on Caerleon Road, Newport. Smith's continued to trade until the early years of the new millennium, operating an interesting and varied selection of buses and coaches.

(John Wiltshire)

Below : Willowbrook was one of a number of coachbuilders to produce single-deck bodies to what was to be known as the BET style. Hundreds of bodies to this design were built on a variety of chassis for a large number of customers including many municipal and independent fleets. Probably the greatest numbers were on Leyland's Tiger Cub and Leopard chassis, and AEC's Reliance. City of Oxford Motor Services was an enthusiastic AEC customer and their last new buses of AEC manufacture were eight Reliance saloons in 1971. The first four had Willowbrook dual-purpose bodies like *SWL51J* in this view. It had been sold by City of Oxford to Surrey operator Gastonia of Cranleigh, and passed to Gwent operator Richards of Nantyglo in October 1982. John Richards started in 1971 and operated some rather unusual coaches including two ex-Black and White Daimler Roadliners with Perkins engines and a rare UTIC-AEC integral. The Reliance is seen in Richards' yard on 9 January 1983 and remained in service until March 1986, when Hampshire-based hippies purchased it for conversion to a caravan. The only other bus owned was a former London Country AEC Swift, *DPD505J*, which lasted less than a year, after which some local gypsies took it away for scrap. The business itself had actually been sold to Morgan of Nantyglo in March 1986, shortly before the departure of *SWL51J*.

(John Jones)

Norman operated out of Oxengate garage in Cwmllynfell and traded as Gwys Luxury Coaches. Cwmllynfell is a small former mining community on the A4068 between Gurnos and Brynamman, perhaps more famous for its rugby club and the views of the Black Mountains to the north. To the south of Cwmllynfell are the remains of a large opencast site. Norman made a bold move in September 1969 when they purchased a six-year-old Guy Wulfrunian *WHL978* from West Riding. It is not known whether it was actually operated but it had been sold for scrap by April 1970. Far more mundane buses to follow were a Willowbrook-bodied Bedford VAL from Wigmore of Dinnington in 1971 which was exported to the Irish Republic in 1977, and a Weymann-bodied Leyland Leopard arrived from Southdown in 1978. Following the acquisition in 1975 of a coach from Yates of Runcorn, that operator's livery was then adopted as standard. In March 1981 *JEH187K* was one of two 1971 ECW-bodied Bristol RESLs acquired, that were new to PMT. The other example being *JEH190K*, that arrived the following year, via Gastonia of Cranleigh. *JEH187K* is seen on the garage forecourt on 24 September 1983. Norman ceased operations in October 1986.

(John Jones)

In this section we look at a selection of buses in action out on the road. Unless they were used on stage carriage work, many privately owned buses only ventured out at certain times of the day and were often parked up all weekend, making anything other than a yard photograph difficult to obtain. By 1969, Rees and Williams were operating both from Swansea and also Llanelli to Llandeilo via Pontardulais and Ammanford. In 1986 the service to Llandeilo from Swansea remained, but that from Llanelli ran only to Ammanford via Tycroes. Rees and Williams' Leopard *WTH338M* is not hanging about as it enters Tycroes and passing Coopers flats on 28 May 1986, it is bound for Llandeilo on

the service from Swansea. Rees and Williams favoured the Leyland Leopard for service bus work in the 1970s and purchased no fewer than five new examples between 1971 and 1974. The first two were bodied by Willowbrook but *WTH338M*, new in October 1973, and subsequent *YBX469/70M* of 1974, had attractive Plaxton Derwent II bodywork. When Rees and Williams sold out in August 1988 to D Coaches of Morriston, all five of these Leopards passed to that fleet for continued use.

(John Jones)

From the mid-1970s former Nottingham buses became very popular on the second-hand market and as dozens of well looked after rear-engined double-deckers became available, it was inevitable that a few would find their way into the hands of Welsh independents. Both Fleetlines and Atlanteans found homes in South Wales and *JTV488E* was a Leyland Atlantean that had been one of a batch of fifteen which Nottingham bought with Metro-Cammell bodies in 1967. When new it had a centre exit, but this was removed before sale by Nottingham. It passed to Waddon of Bedwas in June 1981 for use on school contracts and was sold in 1985. It is seen negotiating the bend in the A470 known as the "Fiddler's Elbow" near Quakers Yard on 13 June 1982, and is wearing Waddon's striking orange and turquoise blue livery that dated back to the start of operations in 1969. At that time Waddon was based in Senghenydd using a small garage in Abertridwr, before making the move to Bedwas in 1977. *JTV488E* was not the first decker owned, though it was the first to be operated. A further eleven double-deckers joined the fleet between 1982 and 1995, four of which were Atlanteans, including former Bournemouth and Rhymney Valley examples. Waddon also specialised in minibus refurbishment and traded as a dealer, before finally ceasing to operate in 1998.

(John Jones)

Cream Line's first Leyland PD2s were four obtained in 1967/8 from Southdown, followed by a pair also with Leyland bodies from Leicester City Transport. When Edinburgh Corporation began to sell off PD2/20 models in the early 1970s, Cream Line ended up purchasing four of these, *LFS423/5/7/60*, which had 62 seat lightweight Metro-Cammell bodywork and dating from 1954. Between 1954 and 1956 Edinburgh had received 200 of these buses as tram replacements. *LFS460* was actually purchased via Riverside of Liverpool, and is seen approaching Tonmawr from Neath on 27 April 1973. These were fairly basic buses but were very well looked after by their first owner and *LFS460* had clocked up twenty years service when finally retired by Cream Line in 1974. Three Leyland PD2s with unusual full fronted bodywork arrived from Blackpool Corporation in June 1975 and stayed for three years, and were followed by three front entrance PD2As, coming from Burnley and Pendle in August 1978. These however proved to be badly corroded and were sold after just four months and did not stay long enough to gain Cream Line's livery. These were the last Titans as the Leyland Atlantean came back into favour for a number of years, commencing with a pair from Nottingham.

(John Wiltshire)

East End (Jones) of Clydach developed a taste for slightly more unusual buses, and besides two Dennis Lolines, had an Albion Aberdonian and a pair of Bristol LHs with two-door ECW bodies. In the 1980s they started to build up a fleet of Seddon RUs. The RU was a Gardner-powered rear engine single-decker and East End's examples all had bodies from Seddons' own body shop, Pennine Coachcraft. The first examples were half a dozen from Burnley and Pendle which started to arrive in 1980, and these were followed by four from Fylde Borough Council in 1983. The Fylde livery made an impression as it was adopted as the fleet livery from this time. A further six were purchased from Darlington in 1991, although it should be stressed that not all were operated at the same time, some of the Burnley examples being used for spares and scrapped after a few years. Former Burnley and Pendle *SHG123K* is seen heading through Ammanford on 18 May 1988 on a contract duty and sporting the Fylde style livery from that era. This bus was out of use by May 1992, but the Seddon RUs continued to run until around 2002. Jones later went on to buy Bristol VRTs from United Counties and adopted a green livery for a while. Operations ceased in July 2002 at which point the fleet contained two rare Dennis Falcon saloons that were new to Hartlepool Borough Transport and a selection of former NBC VRTs and several former Scottish MCW Metrobuses.

(John Jones)

Following the withdrawal of the last Red and White Guy Arab III in 1970, West Wales did not operate double-deckers until 1979 when a Bristol VRT was purchased in order to eliminate duplication on the Swansea service. A Leyland PD2 and two PD3s arrived in 1983 but they did not stay long. The arrival of Leyland Atlanteans, however, did mark a return to double-deck operation. A total of seven were acquired including a rather attractive looking pair from Leicester City Transport with Park Royal bodies and bearing registrations *PBC113/5G*. They were new in 1969 and entered service with West Wales in December 1983 as fleet numbers *96* and *97*. Although still wearing its previous owners' livery, *PBC113G* looks very smart as it coasts down towards Swiss Valley,

Felinfoel, past Mydelfyw Service Station, on 24 April 1984. It is working into Llanelli, having come from Ammanford via Cross Hands, on the service run jointly with South Wales Transport. The sign on the filling station forecourt tells us that petrol is a mere £1.79 a gallon. *PBC115G* had by this time been sold, and *PBC113G* would be withdrawn following an accident on 20 June 1984. West Wales Motors sold out to D Coaches in late summer of 1984 and bus *96* passed to them with the business. D Coaches went on to repair and reinstate *PBC113G* and it continued to work until at least 1994. It survives in July 2009 in preservation with a group based in its original home city of Leicester.

(John Jones)

Midway Motors gets it name from Midway garage in Crymych which is where operator Edwards originally ran some buses including a Guy Vixen and a Sentinel. This was taken over in 1959 by Rees and Phillips and the new business expanded rapidly, Phillips eventually leaving the business in 1969. Crymych incidentally is a small village in north Pembrokeshire on the long-closed Whitland to Cardigan railway line. Many Fords have been purchased for service bus work over the years and have included several former NBC examples. One such bus is *TCY256M*, a Willowbrook-bodied R1014 model, which is seen here outward bound from Cardigan to Crymych on 16 April1982. This bus was one of two owned, the other being *SWN86M*, and one of 35 similar buses purchased by South Wales Transport in 1973/4. The premises at Crymych had for years been used to park withdrawn buses which could then be used for spares and an interesting collection thus resulted as time went by. *TCY256M* was withdrawn by 1992.

(John Jones)

And now a selection of buses photographed in and around town centres. Cardigan Castle which dates from the 12th century forms the backdrop to this shot from June 1973, showing the only AEC Reliance bus that Richards Bros ever operated. *VDV798* was purchased in 1971 and was one of a batch of fourteen 41-seat Reliances bodied by Weymann that entered service in 1957 with Devon General. Although not visible in this view, an unusual feature of these particular vehicles was the offside sliding driver's door, which on a front entrance saloon of this design does seem a little pointless. In the Richards fleet this bus was an AEC in a sea of Bedfords at this time, although a handful of double-deckers were owned over the years to add a little more variety. Two Leyland PD2s, one from Ribble and another from Southdown, were purchased in the 1960s, while the last double-decker owned was ex-City of Oxford Bridgemaster *314MFC*, acquired in March 1974. Richards Bros is still a thriving concern in 2009 and besides a large coaching unit, operates a smart fleet of modern saloons on its services, many of which are now supported by local authority grants.

(Martin Llewellyn - Omnicolour)

A street scene in Carmarthen on 28 May 1975 witnesses two of Eynon's saloons sharing the highway with a Mini, an Austin A40, a Mk1 Ford Cortina and two motorcyclists. Were things really that busy back in 1975? The main subject of the photograph is *LBX548G*, a 1969 Leyland Leopard with a Willowbrook body that Eynon's bought new. It was in fact one of a pair ordered by them, but the other one, to have been *LBX547G*, was cancelled, and was delivered to nearby fleet West Wales Motors as *MBX86H*. Ironically, after sale by West Wales in 1982 to an East Anglian operator, *MBX86H* was back in Wales in 1984 with Eynon's. Incidentally there were also Leyland saloons, registered *LBX549/50G*, but these were never intended for Eynon's, being delivered to Davies Bros and West Wales respectively. Eynon's will always be remembered for its double-deckers, but over the years they did operate a number of interesting saloons as well as coaches. The Leyland Leopard was always a popular choice, with second-hand examples coming from Ribble, Southdown and Greater Manchester PTE. Tiger Cubs were also particularly interesting, with former Fishwick and King Alfred examples being amongst those operated. *LBX548G* remained in service with Eynon's until December 1981, passing to a Barnsley breaker in June 1982 in exchange for three Leyland engines.

(John Jones)

Silcox of Pembroke Dock was very fond of the Bristol LH model and purchased some quite interesting examples over the years in both bus and coach form, new and second-hand. Three identical buses of particular interest came from Greater Manchester PTE of all places in 1982, and were new in 1974. They had 43-seat ECW bodies to a style that pre-dated the year of build, featuring flat fronts, and were originally ordered by Wigan Corporation. Silcox sold one of the trio in September 1983, and this bus, *BNE766N*, passed to Williams and Davies of Betws who traded as Bryncelyn Coaches. They were based at Bryncelyn Garage in Betws which was just to the south-east of Ammanford. The business was started by Williams in 1950 based at Garnswllt with a pre-war Dodge, and was always a very small fleet. In 1956 he moved to Betws and in 1964 a new Bedford VAS was purchased which lasted until 1991, when it was sold for further service. In 1971 Davies joined Williams, and a new livery was adopted in 1980 following the purchase of a minibus from Waddon Coaches of Caerphilly (see page 36). In September 1983 Williams and Davies took over the Ammanford to Garnswllt service from West Wales Motors of Tycroes. *BNE766N* is seen on service in Ammanford on a wet day in March 1986, but nonetheless smartly turned out. The control of Bryncelyn Coaches passed entirely to Davies in 1996.

(Richard Evans)

Coity's routes were always relatively short, requiring only two buses, and in July 1970 they took delivery of what was to become a unique bus. The previous new bus received in 1968, had been *STG185F*, a Plaxton Derwent-bodied Leyland Tiger Cub with dual-purpose seating. Whilst having a similar style Plaxton body, *ATG459H* was in fact an 11-metre Bristol LHL6L, and the only example of an LHL to receive a bus body, in this case with 55 seats. It is seen entering Bridgend town centre on 26 March 1983. Six months later in September most of the Coity fleet including this unique bus would be destroyed in a fire at their garage. Also destroyed would be Tiger Cubs *DNY994C* (see page 61), *STG185F*, and the sole coach Bedford VAM14 *LTG981E*, while Ford R1014 bus *MNY49P* was damaged. The only survivor was rare Burlingham-bodied Tiger Cub *630JNY* of 1961, which today is happily preserved as a reminder of this once fine fleet. After the fire, Coity picked up the pieces and rebuilt its fleet with second-hand buses before selling out to Morris Travel of Pencoed in 1985.

(John Jones)

The Jones of Newchurch business dates back to 1927 when a lorry fitted with seats was introduced on a service from Pontywaun to Carmarthen. Jones were based at Ffoshelig Garage in Newchurch which was situated to the north-west of Carmarthen. By the late 1940s the haulage business had been sold and three routes were now operated out of the town. Deregulation in 1986 brought activity in Carmarthen on town services and by 1990 Jones had interests in up to ten services. The fleet has always been immaculately turned out and for many years vehicles carried a smart blue and cream livery before changing to brown and cream in the 1980s. Bedfords, often bought new, were the choice for many years but Bristol LH and Leyland Leopard buses have also been operated. *WUX658K* is a 1971 Bedford YRQ with a Willowbrook body that was new to Brown of Donnington Wood in Shropshire. It joined the Jones fleet in September 1978 and eventually passed to Richards of Moylegrove in late 1983. It is seen in Carmarthen on 30 December 1978 looking very well cared for. The business continues in 2009 but under the ownership of Rhodri Evans.

(John Jones)

Cream Line of Tonmawr bought its last brand new bus in 1977, a 53-seat Plaxton Derwent-bodied Bedford YMT, and it was also the last of several new Bedfords bought since 1970. However, the majority of service and contract work was in the hands of Leyland Leopards, when in 1980, Cream Line turned to the Leyland Panther, buying four examples of this temperamental beast. Two attractive Plaxton Highway-bodied Leopards arrived from Lancashire United in October 1977. LUT had by this time built up a strong relationship with Plaxton, which would supply them with single-deck bus bodies well into the 1970s. The Creamline pair were registered *DTF586/8B*, had 50 bus seats, and dated from 1964. *DTF588B* is seen leaving Neath Victoria Gardens bus station bound for Pontrhydyfen on 11 February 1978. Pontrhydyfen was a village nestling in the Afan valley and was the birthplace of actor Richard Burton. Note the fleet name Creamline is now one word and how the colour scheme has been applied to take account of Plaxton's decorative beading on this style of body. Despite being well turned out, these two fine vehicles only lasted two years or so.

(John Jones)

Abertillery, by nature of its geographical location, meant that Henley's buses operated over some quite demanding terrain. Seen here descending a typical street of terraced houses in Abertillery on 5 September 1981 while working the Blaenau Gwent service is *XAX448*, an AEC Reliance that started life with neighbouring operator Jones of Aberbeeg. New in 1960 it had Weymann bodywork and passed to Henley's in August 1971, and had been converted to one-man operation by March 1974. It was eventually scrapped in 1983 having donated its bus seats to ex-Western Welsh *WKG287*. Henley's was already operating a couple of Abertillery local services when they took over the

Brynithel - Abertillery - Cwmtillery route from Colliers which was jointly run with Jones of Aberbeeg, at that time. In post-war years buses operated included a number of Bedford OWBs, AEC Regals acquired from fleets such as Llynfi and Gelligaer UDC, as well as a selection of AEC Reliance saloons including one bus and several grant specification coaches purchased new. By the mid-1980s Henley ran four stage carriage services centred around the Abertillery area, and unlike many other operators featured in this book, they still trade in 2009 doing what they have done for many decades.

(John Jones)

A relatively short-lived firm was Appleton of Bridgend which began operating in April 1984 and traded as Ace Coaches, although some vehicles carried the title Ace of Bridgend. From their yard close to the town centre in Bridgend they built up a fleet of four double-deckers, a pair of AEC Reliance saloons and around nine coaches. One of the double-deckers was a Leyland PD3A that started life with Preston Corporation, the other three being Daimler Fleetlines, but nonetheless all were quite interesting examples. Making its way through the narrow side streets in its home town on 29 October 1986 is *KXS716K* which dates from 1972, and was previously working for Heyfordian in Oxfordshire. It was, however, one of a pair of Fleetlines, *KXS715K* being the other, new to Grahams Bus Service of Paisley, both of which passed to Heyfordian in 1979. In March 1986 two local services from Bridgend were registered, an hourly departure to St Brides and a two-hourly to Llantwit Major, on which double-deckers were used. It was short-lived and the services together with four vehicles (including *KXS716K*) passed to Morris Travel of Pencoed in December 1986.

(Andrew Wiltshire)

In the winter months Llynfi Motor Services' main route was from Maesteg to Port Talbot (Bethany Square) via Bryn, a small village high on the hill between Maesteg and the coast, and where Llynfi had a second depot including workshop facilities. In the summer months the service was operated jointly with South Wales Transport and was extended to Aberafan Beach. In August 1975 Llynfi bought two early Leyland Leopards with synchromesh gearboxes from Portsmouth Corporation. They had registrations YBK132/8, Weymann bodies with 42 seats and also had narrow centre exits, which Llynfi immediately removed. After being brought up to Llynfi's high standard, *YBK132* entered service the following month as a 44-seater and carried fleet number *129*. The bus has now been in service for six months with its new owner as we see it leaving Maesteg on 2 March 1976, and heading off on a workers service to the Abbey Works, the massive steel making complex at Port Talbot. This particular bus lasted until July 1988, when Llynfi sold the business to an offshoot of the then-privatised South Wales Transport.

(John Wiltshire)

47

It is now time for a glimpse of competition on the streets of the capital city. Long before most of the UK had seen its bus industry de-regulated in 1986, and witnessed its towns and cities subjected to a new phenomenon, last seen in the 1920s, namely competition, Cardiff had already experienced just this, at first hand in 1981. Keith Morris started out in 1973 with a minibus and CK Coaches (Cardiff) Ltd was formed in 1974, with the business then concentrating on private hire work. Incidentally the name CK was derived from the initials of the proprietors Carol and Keith Morris. Then in 1981 CK obtained temporary licences to operate two routes in the city, the first competition for the Cardiff municipal fleet since 1927. These services commenced on 6 April 1981 and used crew-operated buses and charged lower fares, prompting a "fares war". Some existing buses were made available but five former London Transport Fleetlines were bought specifically for the new enterprise. *THM586M* has made its way along Greyfriars Road and is about to turn into Park Place passing on the corner, the New Theatre. It is bound for Cyncoed on service 54 travelling via City Road. The date is 18 April and the new services have been running for nearly three weeks. Both CK and the City of Cardiff Transport fleet used orange and white as their fleet colour scheme, but CK used a much healthier application of white.

(John Wiltshire)

48

One could well understand CK wanting to get a slice of the action with a service to Llanrumney which is a large and heavily-populated housing estate to the east of Cardiff. Even in 2009, Llanrumney remains a well patronised service for Cardiff Bus. Cyncoed on the other hand seemed an unusual choice of destination, being a wealthy area of high car ownership. In 1980 CK purchased this very traditional Leyland PD3A number *87HBC* from Leicester City Transport. It had an open platform East Lancs body and a respectable seating capacity for 74 passengers. The bus entered service wearing a blue and white overall advert livery for Cardiff's then new local independent radio station CBC. A second half-cab arrived in 1981 from Warrington Borough Council, in the shape of *BED724C*, an unusual 7' 6" wide Leyland PD2 with forward entrance East Lancs bodywork. In the early afternoon of   16 October 1981 we see *87HBC* heading inbound along what is today Stuttgarter Strasse, and making its way to Wood Street. CK did not use the Central bus station, but instead used stands on the north side of Wood Street.

(John Wiltshire)

The main double-deck performers were normally the five *THMxxxM* registered Leyland-engined Fleetlines that came from London Transport and which had 68-seat dual-door bodies by MCW. A sixth Daimler Fleetline would occasionally deputise in the shape of *SOE917H*. This vehicle was purchased back in 1979 and was quite a different bus altogether. It was one of a large batch of 33-foot buses that West Midlands PTE was taking out of service prematurely with serious structural defects. It was a Gardner-engined bus with a Park Royal dual-door body with seating for 80. It carries the earlier CK livery incorporating black relief, and is seen on 18 April 1981 travelling down Kingsway in Cardiff city centre. CK went on to run a further route to Llanedeyrn, but ran into problems in early 1982 and operations ceased on 13 February. They recommenced on 22 February and Swanbrook of Staverton acquired an interest from 1 March, using some of its own buses. However, this only lasted a few more weeks and all CK's licences were revoked on 31 March. CK started up as a coach company once again later that year.

(John Wiltshire)

When introduced from 1953 onwards, the Bristol Lodekka soon became regarded as a solid and reliable bus. It was to become a very popular choice in the early 1970s amongst the South Wales area private operators, and it was of course a low-height bus with a normal seating layout on the upper deck. Large numbers of early examples dating from the 1950s had come on to the second-hand market, most of which had platform doors making them ideal for schools contracts. Morris Bros was very keen on the Bristol marque and took numerous examples of the LS, many of which were coaches from Royal Blue, before progressing onto MW and RE coaches. Early double-deckers taken into stock were a pair of splendid low-bridge layout Bristol KSW5Gs from Southern Vectis (*JDL721/2*), followed by two Bristol LD6Gs from Bristol Omnibus, *UHY409/10*, which were new in 1955. They arrived in August 1971 and were still owned when the fleet expanded dramatically in 1974, at which time a third LD, new to Crosville (*618LFM*), arrived from Rennies of Dunfermline. This view of *UHY409* was taken in the coach park at Porthcawl on 6 July 1974. It was withdrawn during 1976 and passed to a Barnsley breaker in December of that year. Morris subsequently took ten of the later FLF model Lodekkas in 1980 which went on to serve them well into that decade.

(John Jones)

Jenkins of Skewen operated a small number of double-deckers in the 1950s including a pair of Weymann-bodied AEC Regents from Sheffield but all had gone by the end of 1956. The Bristol Lodekka appeared in 1970 when *XFM248* was acquired from Crosville Motor Services, in whose fleet it had been *DLB836*. This tells us that it was a LD6B Bristol-powered model and here we see it parked in the yard on 24 September 1974 looking very smart. It was joined in June 1975 by *OCY957* that had been working for Alder Valley, but was actually new to United Welsh. Both Lodekkas continued to perpetuate the earlier maroon livery, long after the saloons had adopted a yellow and white colour scheme. Incidentally *XFM248* had a single white band, whereas *OCY957* received two yellow bands to its maroon. *XFM248* was withdrawn and sold in 1976, by which time it was 20 years old, while *OCY957* lasted only until the end of 1977 when it was despatched for breaking up, after which no further double-deckers were purchased. In December 1988 the business was sold to Smith Shearings of Wigan which gave this large operator a base in Skewen from which coaches and buses were to be operated for a number of years.

(John Wiltshire)

Hutchins, whose existence was rather brief, was an operator based in Pontardawe, a former steel and tinplate town in the Swansea Valley. Hutchins was fond of Ford coaches and only ever operated four buses. The first was a former Rhondda Tiger Cub *XTG366* which came from Edwards of Talbot Green in 1975. The same year saw the purchase of *TUO500*, the first of a pair of Bristol Lodekkas, followed by an Albion Nimbus (*897BTG*) that was new to Brewer of Caerau. The Lodekkas are both visible in this view at their yard on 27 February 1977. The green bus, *TUO500* is a former Western National example of 1956, whilst in the background is *5666EL* which still carries the poppy red livery of NBC era Hants and Dorset, to whom it was new in 1961. Both are 60-seaters with platform doors, and *TUO500* is an LD6B model, whereas *5666EL* is a later flat-floor FS6B example also with a Bristol engine. Both buses ran un-repainted and were sold by 1977, whilst Hutchins ceased operating in 1978.

(John Jones)

Over the years until the mid-1970s Edmunds of Rassau near Ebbw Vale ran a mouth-watering variety of double-deckers. *ORM143* was a Bristol LD6G, one of a batch of five new to Cumberland Motor Services in 1955 and fitted with the usual ECW body seating 60. It was just one of eleven Lodekkas that passed through the fleet between 1969 and 1976, the other ten however all originating with Crosville. It is seen close to the garage in Rassau on 8 July 1973. *ORM143* was sold the following month to Potter at Skewen near Neath, having only been in the fleet for sixteen months, which was not unusual. Edmunds' first double-decker was an Albion Venturer with a Welsh Metal Industries body purchased new in 1948. Other gems included AEC Regents from London, Liverpool, Oxford and South Wales Transport, Guy Arabs from Birmingham, Southdown and Lancashire United, a pair of Northampton Daimler CVG6s *DNH195/8*, Bristol Ks and Leyland TDs and PDs. Of particular interest was the former AEC Bridgemaster demonstrator *9JML* from Birmingham Corporation Transport and an early Dennis Loline, *SOU469*, from Aldershot and District.

(John Jones)

It is 1981 and is now the John Williams era of Porthcawl Omnibus. Very few independent bus operators can claim to have used on open-topper in normal service, but Porthcawl Omnibus had this convertible Bristol LD6G dating from 1959. *627HFM* was acquired in 1981 from Bristol Omnibus where it would only have its roof removed for a few months in the summer. The bus is seen on Porthcawl Esplanade on 9 August on the service to Rest Bay from Coney Beach and is minus its roof. It was originally new to Crosville Motor Services, as *DLB17*, one of six fitted from new with detachable roofs, and painted cream, for use at Llandudno, Colwyn Bay and Rhyl. *DLB17* was like the majority of Crosville Lodekkas, powered by a Bristol engine, and in 1973 the bus passed to Bristol Omnibus who subsequently fitted a Gardner 6LW engine. *627HFM* then became *L8581* and was put to work in the open-top fleet at Weston-Super-Mare. It was sold by Porthcawl Omnibus in 1991 passing to Monetgrange (Dunn Line) of Nottingham and by 2003, was working for Cumbria Classic Coaches in the Lake District. They were still using the bus for private hire and tours in 2008, and *627HFM* still possessed its detachable roof, and had also acquired a Gardner 6LXB engine in place of the 6LW.

(John Jones)

Swansea-based operator Gordon Fussell was in the PSV business for less than twenty years. Based at Fforestfach in the northern part of the city, he commenced trading in 1959 with a new Bedford CA minibus, and went on to purchase further new minibuses. These were later followed by a pair of new Bedford SBs delivered in 1964 and 1966, and in July 1971 a very interesting vehicle arrived. It was *UHA233*, a BMMO CL3 from Midland Red, which was a rebuilt 1954 C3 chassis with a new Plaxton coach body in the early 1960s. It only stayed for nine months, but in September 1972 Fussell acquired his first and only buses, two Bristol LS5Gs from Bristol Omnibus and a solitary Lodekka from Eastern Counties. The Lodekka is seen here some way from home in Pontypridd in July 1973. *UNG177* was one of the more rare LD5G models and entered service in 1956 as Eastern Counties *LKD177*. The 5-cylinder Gardner 5LW engine was specified by a number of Tilling fleets, usually those serving less demanding terrain such as Lincolnshire Road Car and Eastern National. Eastern Counties only turned to the larger 6LW engine for its thirty foot double-deckers. Fussell's affair with buses was brief and all three Bristols were sold by September 1977, the business going on to cease trading in 1978.

(John Wiltshire)

We now have a selection of buses doing what they were always intended to do, namely picking up passengers. Eynon's faith in the Leyland Titan only really changed with a shift from open-platform rear-entrance buses like the Plymouth pair on page 19, to a preference for the front-entrance variety. Some of these had a sliding door like the PD3A on page 1, while most came with folding platform doors like this former Brighton Corporation Transport example. *BUF529C* was actually one of two Leyland PD2/37s, *BUF528C* being the other, that Brighton had sold to Warrington Corporation Transport in 1978 to help solve a temporary vehicle shortage. They became Warrington *98* and *99*

and when withdrawn and sold, Eynon's snapped up the pair of them in 1980 and put them into service straight away. They both dated from 1965 and had fairly common Weymann 64-seat bodies. *BUF529C* is seen loading passengers in Llanelli on 31 July 1985 in anticipation of the run to Trimsaran and on to either Kidwelly or Carmarthen. As no blind is displayed one cannot be sure of the final destination. This bus was taken out of service the following March and used for spares while *BUF528C* soldiered on until October 1987, passing into non-PSV use by 1988.

(Andrew Wiltshire)

Thomas Motor Services had a history in the Barry area that stretched back to 1914, although in the 1920s there were around 100 other operators in the same town. Thomas lived on as the sole survivor operating a route from Barry to Cardiff via Dinas Powis which uses one of the lower roads, and which was originally jointly run with Western Welsh (later National Welsh) up until deregulation. Buses used in post-war years included a variety of pre-war Leyland Tigers, an ex-Birmingham Daimler COG5 (*EOG182*) and a pair of ex-Burton-upon-Trent Guy Arab III saloons, to name but a few. In 1959 a new Leyland Tiger Cub, *670BTX* with a distinctive Duple Midland body was purchased and lasted until August 1970, when this rather attractive Leyland Leopard, *ATG708J* arrived. This had a BET style Willowbrook 53-seat body and was unusual as it had a full rear destination display. It too saw just over eleven years of service and was withdrawn in January 1982. The bus was sold to a dealer in Fareham who scrapped the body and exported the chassis to Australia in May 1982, where it was bodied locally as a coach. *ATG708J* was replaced by a new Leopard coach and Thomas continued to operate the service using coaches until a used Leyland National appeared in 1989. This view taken on 8 December 1973 shows the bus in Cardiff bus station about to depart once again for its home town.

(John Jones)

Prior to World War II the Leyland Titan had been the favoured choice of double-decker for Rees and Williams. During the war three Guy Arab utilities arrived, two being Arab II models which were later rebodied by Burlingham in 1950. Further Guy Arab IIs arrived in 1946 and 1948, both of which were rebodied in the 1950s, whilst 1947 saw the arrival of a Leyland Titan PD1A. Three Guy Arab IVs with lowbridge Massey bodies were to be the last new double-deckers for this operator. The final example was delivered in 1962 as *YTH815* and featured the unusual "Johannesburg" bonnet and radiator grill. It is seen here in Llanelli in September 1967 and wearing the original livery, and would be working the Llandeilo service 16 (later to become 104), which was operated jointly with South Wales Transport. Worth noting is the spelling "Llanelly" on the route blind. This is the Anglicised form which until about 1965 was used on government and official documents. Needless to say, the blinds were eventually changed to the more acceptable Welsh version. *YTH815* was sold in 1977 and went on to serve Warstone Motors in Staffordshire well into the 1980s. It was then returned to Wales for preservation in the Llanelli area, and still exists, although in very poor condition, at the Pembrey Country Park.

(Martin Llewellyn - Omnicolour)

As a new purchase, the Bristol LH with ECW bus body was a fairly rare beast outside of the National Bus Company. However, a total of five were acquired by two operators in the Carmarthen area between 1972 and 1977. The LH was a lightweight bus, and given that the Tiger Cub had been phased out by Leyland, perhaps it was no real surprise that Dan Jones had four of these together with a single Plaxton Derwent-bodied example to add variety. The first one was *RBX565K* followed by two identical buses, *XTH501/2M*, in 1974. They had 45 seats and carried fleet numbers *21* and *22*, respectively. Number *21* is seen loading passengers in Carmarthen on 28 May 1975. All of Dan Jones' LHs passed to Davies Bros on 1 April 1978 and *XTH501M* became number *114* with its new owner. It was withdrawn after only nine years service in 1983, and then waited a further fourteen years before it passed to a Swansea scrap dealer in 1997.

(John Jones)

The final three double-deckers purchased by Creamline of Tonmawr marked a change from the previous Leyland Atlanteans. They were Daimler Fleetlines that were new to London Transport but did have Leyland engines though. *GHV22* and *982N* had Park Royal bodies and had been rebuilt to single door layout at some stage, whereas *KUC984P*, seen here on 8 March 1986, has an MCW body and dates from 1976. The location is Neath bus station and the smartly turned out vehicle claims to be going to Skewen via Neath Abbey. A blind has been fitted but seems a little lost in the existing destination box. Creamline ceased operations suddenly on 30 January 1987. The previous autumn there had been a serious incident when former Southampton Atlantean *OCR151G* went off the road and down an embankment at Pontrhydyfen, which attracted a lot of bad publicity, and may have prompted the owners of Creamline to retire from the bus business. The services subsequently passed to South Wales Transport. The three Fleetlines passed to the Capitol Group together with an Atlantean and a quartet of Leyland Panthers that Creamline had amassed before they ceased. *KUC984P* eventually ended up in the United States employed on sightseeing tours.

(Andrew Wiltshire)

Leylands were probably the most common type of bus purchased by independents in the area and most types featured at one time or another. Here is a varied selection. When *HPT324H* migrated from Durham independent Trimdon Motor Services to the Dan Jones fleet in Carmarthenshire in 1974 it was a relatively new bus at just four years old. It was one of a batch of six similar buses, *HPT320-5H*, new in 1970, and by coincidence the other five all found new homes in South Wales in 1974. Cream Line of Tonmawr had a trio including dual-purpose seated *HPT325H*, whilst Llynfi and R I Davies took one each

of the remaining pair. *HPT324H* was a rather fine looking Plaxton Derwent II-bodied Leyland Leopard and was given fleet number *14* in the Jones fleet. Upon transfer to Davies Bros of Pencader in April 1978 with the Jones business, it became *107* and eventually gained this attractive red and cream livery. It is seen laying over at Llandeilo on a pleasant 27 January 1982. After a further fifteen years service with Davies it was withdrawn in June 1997 and had passed to the British Bus Preservation Group by August 1999. It is thought to have been scrapped subsequently.

(John Jones)

David and Sylvia Letherby came from Trebanog, a small community that developed along a road in the Rhondda, high up on the hillside between Tonyrefail and Porth. They adopted the fleet-name Cambrian Coaches, when they entered the coach business in 1975 by purchasing an unusual Reading-bodied Bedford VAS coach from CK of Cardiff. For many years they ran only coaches including AEC, Bedford, Seddon and Volvo and they only ever operated two buses. These were a Strachan-bodied Bedford VAM (originally with Wilts and Dorset) and this rather smart looking Massey-bodied Leyland Leopard *STX217G*, which they purchased from Rhymney Valley in January 1984. It is seen on 26 May 1985 in Trebanog and lasted with Letherby for only two years. It was originally new to Caerphilly UDC as their number *17*, one of a dual-door pair delivered in 1968, and carried one of the very last Massey bodies to be built. It was later rebuilt to single door by Rhymney Valley DC.

(John Jones)

After the entry into the fleet in 1965 of its first double-deckers, R I Davies went on to acquire quite an interesting selection of vehicles over the subsequent ten years. These included Bristol Lodekkas, Guy Arabs and a large number of Leyland PD2s from various sources including Blackpool, Bolton and Barrow-in-Furness. Most were repainted into fleet livery but rarely saw more than two years service before being sold for scrap. *EHG827* was a rather fine East Lancs-bodied Leyland PD2/12 new to Burnley, Colne and Nelson Joint Transport Committee in 1956. It is seen on 18 April 1973 passing Merthyr's modern fire station and heading for either Trefechan or going all the way to Pontsticill. Two stage carriage services were operated from Merthyr which used both double-deckers and saloons. One route ran to Trefechan and on to Pontsticill via Cefn Coed whilst the other was a joint operation with Merthyr Tydfil (alternate 3-month periods throughout the year), that terminated at the Cefn Hotel in Cefn Coed. At the time of this photograph Merthyr Tydfil was operating this service in accordance with its April-June rostered period.

(John Jones)

Coity Motors began trading in 1924 with a service from the village of Coity to nearby Bridgend. Coity was a mere two miles to the north east of Bridgend and its main attraction, buses aside, was Coity Castle, the ruins of a Norman castle with later additions dating from the 14th century. The proprietor of this business was a Mr D John and over the years a variety of buses were operated including those of Morris, Guy, Commer, Bedford and Leyland manufacture, all before World War II. After the war, new Leyland buses started to appear and featured a pair of Burlingham-bodied Tigers, a Leyland-bodied Royal Tiger and several Tiger Cubs. DNY994C is a Tiger Cub, new in March 1965, the fifth such example to be purchased new, and which featured a Willowbrook body with dual-purpose seating for 41. It is seen here in picturesque Coity on 4 August 1975. By 1969 Coity operated three services out of Bridgend, two of which ran via Coity.

(John Wiltshire)

Right : Llynfi Motor Services did not acquire their first double-deckers until 1957 when a pair of attractive Massey-bodied Daimler CVD6s were purchased from Oxfordshire independent Heyfordian. The following year a brand new Leyland PD3/4 was placed into service. It is thought it may have been an experimental chassis that was purchased at a reduced price before bodying. Carrying fleet number *72* it was registered *YTG304* and had a Massey 72 seat front-entrance body with a sliding entrance door. What made it particularly interesting is that when it was new, it was painted silver with three blue bands. It gained normal fleet livery in the early 1960s and was to remain on fleet strength for just over twenty nine years. During its time with Llynfi *YTG304* would normally be used on workers' services and had its regular driver for many years. This view on 20 August 1976 breaks the mould as the bus is seen leaving Maesteg for Aberavon Beach (the English spelling), and will climb steeply out of the town centre and on towards Port Talbot and ultimately Aberafan. After leaving Llynfi, *YTG304* became a mobile advertisement hoarding for Bevington Motors at Margam in 1987, and was eventually sold for use as a luxury mobile caravan for Double Deck Tours (Peter Garforth) and undertook tourists holidays in Yorkshire. It subsequently passed into preservation with an owner in Sussex.

(John Wiltshire)

Below : Another well-known operator in the Bridgend area for many years was Humphries whose grey and red vehicles always provided a wealth of interest for the enthusiast. Operations began in 1948 and buses featured in the fleet from these early years included an ex-South Shields Daimler COG5 and a number of Bedford OWBs. Only two buses were operated in the 1960s, but the following decade saw quite a variety starting with *99ATX*, a Willowbrook-bodied Tiger Cub from Coity Motors, and *WKG287*, an AEC Reliance from Western Welsh. Two Tiger Cubs from Western Welsh were *JBO110* of 1954 and Willowbrook-bodied *MKG480* of 1956 that had dual-purpose seating. The newer bus had come via a contractor in Port Talbot and is seen here on 22 July 1973 at Humphries' Brackla yard dominated by Nissen huts. *MKG480* was later fitted with bus seats and eventually sold for conversion to a caravan in 1976. In 1970 Humphries briefly operated two local services that had been abandoned by Western Welsh but coaches were used, and during the 1970s the bus fleet was confined to contract work. Operations ceased in July 1980 when Humphries sold the business to Morris Travel of Pencoed.

(John Jones)

Having picked up a large number of schools contracts that it is believed were previously in the hands of South Wales Transport, D Coaches would need to get their hands on a large number of used double-deckers fairly quickly. So in December 1975 they purchased eighteen quite elderly Leyland PD2s from Lothian Regional Transport followed by a further eleven in February 1976. All twenty nine buses had Metro-Cammell lightweight bodies most seating 63 passengers, and joined identical bus *LFS423* (see page 16). Two were new in 1954, the remainder in 1955 and would have been obtained at a very good price, most probably via a Barnsley dealer. Two of these buses were never

licensed and it must be assumed were used for spares, and none was ever repainted into fleet livery, either being touched up or given a fresh coat of madder and white. *LWS540* seen here on 22 February 1976 at Llansamlet, and surrounded by similar looking buses, was to survive until August 1979 when it was sold for scrap. The story does not end there, as in January 1977 D Coaches bought ten front-entrance Leyland PD3s with Alexander bodies from Lothian, which added just a little more variety to the fleet.

(John Wiltshire)

We shall now take a look at various buses lying in their owner's yard at a time when one never knew when something new would appear. A small but well-established firm was that of Phillips who were based in Penrhiwceiber, a mining community at the lower end of the Cynon Valley not far from Abercynon. They ran their first double-decker in 1964, an ex-Ribble Leyland PD2 which was followed by *STG869*, Rhondda Transport's first AEC Regent V of 1956. The Ribble bus was acquired for a works service to the Hirwaun Industrial Estate, but it would appear all subsequent double-deckers were also required for schools work in the area. A further five half-cabs were purchased which included AEC Regent V *VTX437* and Leyland PD3 *CHB411D*. They are seen basking in the sunshine in Phillips' roadside yard at Penrhiwceiber on 6 July 1979. The Regent V on the left came from Morris Bros at Swansea, but had been working for a couple of operators in Scotland after sale by Rhondda Transport in 1972, who bought the bus new in 1957. It has a Weymann body with seating for seventy. On the right we have *CHB411D*, one of two former Merthyr Tydfil Leyland PD3s with East Lancs bodywork which operated for Phillips between 1976 and 1986. After running a number of Atlanteans the Phillips business was to cease operating in September 1997.

(John Wiltshire)

At Tycroes the West Wales Motors depot consisted of a garage with workshop facilities on the roadside (see page 20) with a large yard at the rear. This is where we find *56* (*GTH600E*) on 1 November 1975. The service detailed on the destination blind (Llanelli to Ammanford), was until 1962 operated jointly with James of Ammanford and before 1960 also with Western Welsh. During the 1950s West Wales went to Guy Motors for a number of saloons as well as double-deckers, and purchased Arab UF and LUF models, although only one, *LTH420*, put in a decent number of years service. In 1962 a splendid 36-foot Leopard with Willowbrook 55-seat body, *600ABX*, entered service, and is believed to have been the first saloon of this newly-permitted length to appear in South Wales. A similar chassis was purchased in 1967, the subject of this photograph, and received a much more modern looking Plaxton Derwent II body. Further new buses would include a Leyland Tiger Cub and a Leopard in 1969 followed by further Plaxton-bodied Leopards between 1970 and 1972. *GTH600E* received a two-speed rear axle from a withdrawn former Trent Leopard in 1980, but despite this enhancement was sold in 1982 for non-PSV use in the London area.

(*John Wiltshire*)

It was quite an acceptable practice for a rural operator to store or perhaps abandon, for want of a better word, their redundant vehicles in an adjacent field where they would often remain for years. However here we have a firm that actually ran their buses from a meadow for a number of years. W H Collins began operations in 1965 with a Bedford minibus and had progressed to a 29-seat coach by 1970. Collins was a true West Wales firm being based in Roch, which lies on the main road between St Davids and Haverfordwest, and not far from the breathtaking beach at Newgale. He took over the Haverfordwest to St Davids service in January 1971 after Western Welsh had given it up and left the area. For this operation a variety of second-hand buses was acquired including seven Tiger Cubs of which a pair came from both North Western and Trent. A single 44-seat Leyland Olympian bus, *LKG228*, arrived in January 1972 from Parfitts of Rhymney Bridge having been sold by Western Welsh in 1971. It is seen in Collins "yard" on 2 June 1973, and was one of five buses that passed to Marchwood Motorways (see page 69) in September 1973 when Collins surrendered the bus service and a number of major contracts. Remarkably *LKG228* served Marchwood for a further five years by which time it completed 22 years service. Collins subsequently continued as an operator of minibuses until selling the business in 2009.

(*John Jones*)

Looking very similar to a batch of buses that operated for Western Welsh up until the early 1970s, this AEC Regent V came from the magnificent Maidstone and District fleet. It was a MD3RV model with an AEC AV470 engine and was one of a batch of fourteen similar buses with 59-seat high-bridge layout bodies by Park Royal delivered in 1956. On its way to John Lewis's fleet which it joined in November 1973, *VKR480* had operated in Cornwall for a while with Ede of Par, who had about five of this particular batch of buses. Having platform doors made it an attractive vehicle for school contracts, on which it was used by Lewis along with another AEC Regent V (*DHD184*), of Hebble Motor Services origin, which had a Metro-Cammell body and front entrance. Despite the odd dent *VKR480* still looks good for its 19 years, and is seen parked on the ramp at John Lewis's Morriston yard on 3 June 1975. In 1976 Lewis acquired a further two Park Royal-bodied Regent Vs, this time from East Kent, but to a less pleasing, more angular design and with front entrances.

(John Wiltshire)

66

A second company to be found based in Skewen near Neath was Len Potter, whose business commenced in the 1930s, his first new bus being *TG7785*, a Leyland Cub of 1934. A Duple bus-bodied Bedford OB arrived in 1947 but all subsequent new purchases were coaches, many of which were quite interesting. The only double-decker known to have been operated was *GWE736*, a Leyland TD5 of Sheffield origin, between 1950 and 1954, although a Lodekka arrived in 1973 but was not used. The early 1970s saw the arrival from Western Welsh of a Leyland Olympian *LKG222* and a pair of Bristol saloons.

These were *861RAE*, a rare Bristol SUS from Bristol Omnibus and *487AFM*, this Bristol LS6G of 1956. It has 41 dual-purpose seats and was new to Crosville as *UG338*. It was however purchased from Durber of Stoke in January 1973. It is seen in the depot yard on a sunny 28 July 1973 in the company of *ODW817*, a 1958 Bedford SB3 that had been new to Diaper of Newport. *487AFM* was sold for scrap in November 1976 and Len Potter ceased to trade at the end of August 1977.

(John Jones)

As previously mentioned on page 17, former SWT driver Peter Smith commenced operations in the Ammanford area in 1971. He set up his base at Garnswllt, a small settlement between Ammanford and Pontardulais, from which to operate his newly-acquired services. The Smith fleet operated an interesting collection of saloons which included a number of Bristol LS and MW models as well as an Albion Nimbus and a pair of fairly modern Seddon buses, (YRF136/7H), that had come from Green Bus of Rugeley via Midland Red. The double-deck fleet only ever ran to six buses, by August 1973, comprising ex-Eastern Counties Lodekka UNG178 and five ex-East Yorkshire AEC Bridgemasters (4700/2/3/7/8AT) of 1961, with Beverley Bar roof profiles, and which Smith re-seated from 73 to 75. All double-deckers were smartly turned out in a cream livery with a red band, but by 1975 a number of saloons had appeared in brown and green. In March 1974 three of the Bridgemasters were burnt out in a fire in the yard, and a fourth 4700AT was badly damaged and later sold for scrap. The only survivor was 4708AT which later passed to G&G of Leamington Spa by June 1975 via a dealer in Cheltenham. Before its sale it is seen in the yard at Garnswllt on 26 July 1974 with the fire-damaged 4700AT in the background.

(John Jones)

Thomas of Llangadog purchased their first bus in 1925 and were operating two services by 1931. The firm remained small until 1969 when they took over the services of a family friend, namely LCW Motor Services of Llandeilo. With this business came some substantial services from Llandeilo to places such as Lampeter and Carmarthen and a garage in Llandeilo. In May 1975 Thomas purchased a very interesting bus, a 36-seat Bristol SUL4A registered JNV305D, formerly United Counties 305. The Bristol SU had been developed by Bristol as a replacement for the SC model and came in two lengths, the 28-foot SUL and shorter SUS. It was 7ft 6in wide and had an Albion 4.1 Litre engine mounted under-floor and coupled to a David Brown gearbox. It was built between 1960 and 1966 and JNV305D was the last SU type to be built. It was delivered to United Counties in July 1966 but for some reason did not enter service at Leighton Buzzard until February 1968. It worked for Thomas on schools contracts in the Carmarthenshire countryside until March 1979, when it became a store shed at their Llandeilo depot and its final fate is unknown. It is seen on 23 April 1978 parked in an un-made lay-by near Cil-y-cwm, about 4 miles north of Llandovery, most probably between school journeys. Thomas still trades in 2009 and has operated many interesting buses since 1969.

(John Jones)

Marchwood Motorways of Totton near Southampton gained a contract at Milford Haven in early 1972 and set up a base at Solva, but later moved to Merlyn's Bridge in Haverfordwest. A mixture of vehicles was operated, the older examples tending to be used for site transport with buses being hired from other local operators to meet any short term demand. In September 1973 the stage services and oil refinery contracts of Collins, Roch, were acquired together with most of the vehicles. Marchwood now had the St Davids to Haverfordwest service together with the Haverfordwest to Dale, and Dale to Milford Haven services, for which a number of new Bedford buses were purchased. However operations ceased in August 1981 and the services passed to Richards Bros at this time. This view was taken at the St Davids outstation on 16 September 1978 and shows former Reading Corporation AEC Reliance *SRD20* which had just been purchased from Barry's Coaches of Weymouth. It dates from 1959 and has a Burlingham dual-door body.

(John Jones)

As well as two former City of Oxford AEC Regent Vs, the Morris Bros fleet boasted this splendid 1964 vintage AEC Renown which they obtained from GP Coaches of Longton near Preston in 1975, but which had been new as City of Oxford *345*. The Renown was AEC's successor to their Bridgemaster model (see pages 68 and 72), but had a separate chassis and could receive bodywork by a coachbuilder of the customer's choice. *345TJO*, like most Oxford Renowns was, a 27ft 6in version and had a Park Royal body. Surprisingly it was to remain the only Renown in the Morris Bros fleet, the only other examples with a South Wales independent in the 1970s being three former Western Welsh vehicles that spent a brief period with Morris Travel of Pencoed. *345TJO* became a seat store with Morris by June 1981 and was later sold for preservation, but subsequently became used as a source of spare parts for similar Oxford Renown *340TJO* at the Oxford Bus Museum. In more recent times it is believed to be in the hands of a preservationist in the Halifax area.

(John Wiltshire)

Llynfi Motor Services purchased Coity Motors' first two Leyland Tiger Cubs when they came onto the market. Both were very similar vehicles with two-speed rear axles and Willowbrook bodies with 41 dual-purpose seats. *RTG286* was Coity's first Tiger Cub and dated from June 1955, passing to Llynfi in February 1967, to be joined at Maesteg in 1970 by *VTX44*. Most vehicles in the Llynfi fleet normally gained fleet numbers at some stage, *RTG286* carrying *103* for a short while before settling for *101*. *VTX44* on the other hand did not get a fleet number at all during its six years with Llynfi. The elaborate body trim on *RTG286* stands out well in this view, and the bus is generally looking very smart when it was photographed at its owner's Maesteg yard on 18 November 1979. Sadly, twelve months later, and at the grand old age of 25, it would make a one-way trip to Barnsley and the breaker's torch.

(John Jones)

The "school run" was the main reason there were so many second-hand double-deckers working for the Independent fleets in South Wales. This was brought about because large numbers of children needed to transported, often considerable distances to school, and in particular to high schools. D Coaches was one operator that for a number of years specialised in school contracts. In November 1973 they acquired a pair of slightly more unusual Bristol Lodekkas (*210/1BPU*) from Scottish owner Allander of Milngavie. New to Eastern National in 1954, they were early LD5G models with open platforms which were comparatively rare on Lodekkas. However, Eastern National did have 137 such vehicles delivered between 1954 and 1959, some having Bristol engines. On 22 February 1976 *210BPU* is seen standing in the Llansamlet yard which D Coaches started to occupy from late 1975, due to a dramatic expansion in fleet size, the main workshop facilities remained a mile or so away in Morriston. Clearly visible is the open platform which looks a little odd on this style of bus, and also the remnants of the original deep radiator grill as featured on early Lodekkas of 1953/4 vintage. Both *210* and *211BPU* were sold for scrap in February 1977 after nearly 23 years on the road.

(John Wiltshire)

The second and final double-decker to figure in the Prance fleet was rather interesting to say the least. Being an AEC Bridgemaster was enough to make it a little more unusual, but *TUH363* was a former Cardiff bus that had returned to its native city. It was one of six Bridgemasters new to Cardiff Corporation in 1960 bought primarily for the Tredegar and Merthyr Tydfil services, and all had been sold by early 1972. Five of them passed to Newton of Dingwall (north of Inverness), and after a short while four of them gradually moved south again. *TUH363* thus had an equally brief spell with Walker of Broughty Ferry near Dundee before turning up with Prance of Cardiff in May 1974. Here it received their rather splendid, from a distance, yellow and white livery and saw some use on contract work in and around the city. The bus is seen here in Adam Street late in the afternoon of 11 June 1974, parked just around the corner from their garage and yard in Godfrey Street, and behind the bus looms the boundary wall of H M Prison in Cardiff. In fairly predictable Prance fashion, the Bridgemaster did not stay in the fleet for long, and with the paint barely dry, was sold to an operator deep in north-west Yorkshire by October the same year.

(John Wiltshire)

Cardiff was home to a handful of mainly very small coach operators from the 1960s and into the 1980s. One of the larger fleets was Greyhound with around a dozen coaches, some of which were purchased new, and all employed on contract or private hire work. They wore a smart blue and ivory livery and had a modern garage with a yard at Ely Bridge in the west of the city. In August 1980 they bought their first bus, a smart Northern Counties-bodied Daimler Fleetline of 1968 from City of Nottingham. *MTO125F* was a dual door bus with 72 seats, and would be used for schools contracts, which formed an important part of the Greyhound business at this time. By 1985 it had been repainted into a revised livery with just two narrow cream bands, but still looked very smart. A few weeks into the new school year on 19 September 1986, and *MTO125F* is seen on Llanedeyrn Road about to turn right into the lay-by outside St.Teilo's High School whereupon it will collect its passengers and head for Llanrumney, Trowbridge and St Mellons. This was to be Greyhound's one and only double-decker and the business eventually sold out to Wheadon Coaches.

(Andrew Wiltshire)

In 1970 a small operator Grove Coaches (Barry) Ltd started up in that town, undertaking mainly school contract work and in 1971 local firm Famlitax of Barry was bought out together with four coaches. Early buses included two Plaxton-bodied AEC Reliances from OK Motor Services of Bishop Auckland, and *PEP380*, a rare Yeates Pegasus-bodied Bedford SB5 bus from Mid Wales Motorways of Newtown. In 1976 the company name was changed to Coastal Continental Coach Hire Ltd and in 1981 the first two double-deckers arrived in the form of *MDW390G* and *PDW97H* from Newport Borough Transport. Both were Alexander-bodied Leyland Atlanteans and would be used on school contracts usually to the Cardiff area. They are both seen resting between duties on 12 November 1982, *MDW390G* nearest the camera, at Glantaf High School (Ysgol Gyfun Glantaf) in Llandaff North, Cardiff. Subsequent double-deckers included a pair of Fleetlines from WMPTE and two Bristol VRTs from Cardiff Bus. The livery used soon changed from red and cream to brown and cream, and by the time Coastal ceased to trade in 2008, dark blue was the order of the day.

(John Jones)

Glyn Millington was a former driver with Western Welsh when he started to operate minibuses in 1971 from a base at Kenfig Hill to the west of Bridgend. By 1972 larger coaches had been added to his business including an AEC Reliance, and as the fleet grew in size the operating base was moved to Mountain View Garage at nearby Cefn Cribwr. The fleet name G.M. was later adopted and the first bus to appear was this Leyland PD2/40 in 1981. The appearance of *GWO351C* for use on school contracts heralded the start of a long line of double-deckers acquired for this purpose. The PD2 was a 1965 model with lowbridge Massey bodywork and had come from the Blackwood-based Islwyn Borough Transport municipal fleet, and it is seen in the confines of G.M.'s yard on 31 December 1983. Many double-deckers have been added over the years consisting of mainly Atlanteans, including those of Nottingham and Tyne and Wear origin and VRTs from former NBC fleets. Stage services were briefly operated in 1984 and then more successfully from 1991 for a period, serving Bridgend and Porthcawl. The fleet still operates in 2009 but is linked to the EST Group, and Volvo Citybuses and MCW Metrobuses currently form the double-deck fleet. As for *GWO351C* it is believed that after sale by G.M., the bus was exported to either Belgium or the Netherlands.

(Andrew Wiltshire)

Our next section depicts vehicles which are not quite what they seem. Often buses and coaches are substantially rebuilt or even re-bodied and it can be difficult at first glance to tell exactly what has taken place. The registration mark sometimes offers a clue, depending on whether the transformed vehicle is re-registered. We shall take a look at three such buses, the first of which retained its original registration mark. Hills of Tredegar took delivery of Leyland Tiger Cub NAX537 in January 1955, and it was a rather splendid looking coach with a Burlingham Seagull body with 41 seats. However the vehicle was involved in a serious accident in November 1962 which resulted in the body being scrapped. In 1963, instead of fitting a new coach body to this eight year old chassis, it was decided to send it to Willowbrook at Loughborough to receive bus bodywork to enable it to be used for local service work. As such NAX537 re-entered service in July 1963 and continued to work until March 1975 when it was placed in store. It is seen at Hills depot the previous year on 22 September 1974, giving no clue as to how it looked back in 1955. The bus was brought back into use in October 1977 and served Hills for a further twenty months before being sold.

(John Jones)

This R I Davies saloon could be just another J-registration BET style Leyland Leopard, and is seen entering the bus station at Merthyr on 15 November 1972. However, closer inspection reveals that *YAX474J* is fitted with a Tiger Cub badge and this may arouse suspicion. This re-incarnation is in fact an amalgam of two buses with a new body fitted to finish the job off. The chassis is that of former Grey Green Leyland Tiger Cub *SJJ304* with Harrington centre entrance bodywork that Davies acquired in 1965. It was only used until the following year and soon became derelict. In 1967 Davies took delivery of new a Tiger Cub with Plaxton 45-seat coach bodywork, *LWO314E*, but this vehicle was badly damaged in an accident in June 1970. The body of *SJJ304* was then scrapped, its chassis was refurbished and fitted with the running units of *LWO314E*. The result was then despatched to Willowbrook for the fitting of a new 45-seat body to dual-purpose specification, entering service in August 1971. *YAX474J* was sold to Soudley Valley Coaches in the Forest of Dean in 1974 where it lasted until 1989.

(John Jones)

There were many weird and wonderful creations at Silcox of Pembroke Dock in the 1950s and 1960s that were focussed around new or refurbished Bristol chassis. These included a number of K6G double-deckers, the last of which did not enter service until 1954. Some had second-hand bodies, while other Bristols were rebodied or rebuilt in various ways. Some of this work was done "in-house" by Silcox, and although it may have been sound, this could best be described as basic. The bus in this view, *702RDE* does not really give any clue as to what it is, or for that matter what it might have been in the past. It was in fact based upon the chassis of *DDB270*, a former North Western Bristol L5G/Windover coach, and as well as some new parts, may also have incorporated components from L5G *BJA442*. The "new" chassis was completed in 1962 and was sent to Marshall of Cambridge to receive this rather plain looking full-fronted body, fitted with 39 dual-purpose seats. It was placed into service in April 1963 and served Silcox until September 1973, when it was sold for scrap to Bill Way, the Cardiff dealer and breaker. The bus was parked in the yard at Pembroke Dock on 24 August 1970 for this photograph, and *702RDE* was the last of the Silcox rebuilds to survive.

(John Jones)

"Power from behind". It was inevitable that the rear-engined bus would eventually appear in some of the fleets of South Wales independents during the 1970s, but they did so only in relatively small numbers. This bus had the distinction of being the first Daimler Fleetline with a South Wales area independent and was to be the only rear-engined double-decker purchased by Morris Bros in the 1970s. *BRF733E* began life in 1967 in Staffordshire with the small Potteries area independent Turner of Brown Edge, the first of eight Fleetlines bought new by this operator. It had a Northern Counties body with seating for 73, and having been replaced at Turners by a similar vehicle, it was a relatively modern bus to appear on the second-hand market in 1975. Morris Bros snapped it up and out-shopped it in this rather smart variation of their fleet livery. Its stay in South Wales was short-lived as in 1977 it was sold to well known Doncaster area independent Leon Motor Services of Finningley who numbered it *91* in their fleet. It is seen about to leave Morris's yard on a balmy 25 June 1976.

(John Wiltshire)

Williams of Garnant ran a small fleet of coaches until the arrival of their first bus in 1976, *537JHU*, an ex-Bristol Omnibus Bristol MW5G. Garnant is approximately five miles east of Ammanford, and was originally a mining community that could also boast a small tinplate works. Lying to the south of the Black Mountains, its base was not that far from that of Gareth Evans at Brynamman (see page 79) and also Norman of Cwmllynfell (see page 34). Williams traded as Dericks Coaches, and the MW was followed by *ECN17E*, a former Northern General Leopard and four rather fine ECW-bodied Bristol REs, all of which were turned out in a smart livery of green, white and red, the colours of the Welsh flag. These included *LDL934G*, a 1968 RESL with a flat front, and *SVO96L* a 1973 former East Midland RELH model. The remaining pair were former PMT RELL examples, and *PVT183L* is seen here visiting Cardiff on 6 February 1982, and is parked at the City's Sophia Gardens. The last full-size bus ran for Williams in 1990, after which they operated only minibuses until finally ceasing to trade in 1996.

(John Jones)

Brynamman is a small town in the upper Amman Valley nestling in the southern foothills of the Black Mountains which are part of the Brecon Beacons National Park. In 1961 Gareth Evans started a business using premises vacated by F & E B Russell, just on the Glamorgan side of the border with Carmarthenshire. His early purchases were Commer Avenger and Ford coaches, the first buses being ex-Western Welsh Olympian *LKG227* and a former Yorkshire Traction Tiger Cub, *SVH355*. Of particular interest were *PCY622* an Albion Aberdonian with Plaxton bus body new to LCW of Llandeilo and *GTC105F*, a 1967 Leyland Panther with an East Lancs body. The Panther was one of half a dozen similar vehicles purchased by Lancaster City Transport in 1967/8, and is seen here at Evans premises on 10 June 1981 having been purchased nearly two years earlier. This vehicle lasted until 1987, which is quite impressive for a Leyland Panther. Evans went on to own an early model Leyland National (*OVO562L*) of East Midland origin, his last bus, and eventually in May 1996 sold his business to K & S Davies, who in 2009 are still trading from Evans' former premises.

(John Jones)

Burrows of Ogmore Vale was started by two brothers shortly after World War II and their first vehicle was a trusty Bedford OB soon followed by a Dennis Lancet, both bought new. Further coaches arrived throughout the 1950s and 1960s and in 1976 the first double-decker was purchased, an early Leyland Atlantean that had been new to Liverpool Corporation. By the late 1970s further buses included an Albion Lowlander from Western SMT and some Leyland Panthers including a pair from Burnley and Pendle. In 1979 an Atlantean, *END828D*, and a solitary Fleetline, *DNF718C*, both with MCW bodies and new to Manchester Corporation Transport arrived from Greater Manchester PTE. A further Atlantean, *END823D*, arrived in April 1980, and all three were repainted into Burrows white and blue livery with initials RDB as a fleet name, as seen here on *END823D*. This view was taken on a rather overcast 26 February 1983, and was a stroke of luck, as Burrows yard was quite small and vehicles were usually packed in tightly, making photography very difficult. Burrows originally used their buses for mining and works contracts, but with the decline of industry in the area school contracts became the mainstay, until 1991 when a stage service was operated for a while.

(John Jones)

In October 1975 Brewers of Caerau took a quartet of these Alexander-bodied AEC Swifts from City of Cardiff Transport. These thirty-six-foot buses were the first rear-engined vehicles for Brewers and also the first with a dual-door layout, a feature which Brewers was to retain. They gave good service in the Llynfi Valley and when sold in March 1983, *MBO516/8F* passed to John at Llanharry. This small and relatively short-lived firm had started out in 1973 as K M John and was primarily a coach operating concern. It became K & P John in 1976 and the first bus arrived in 1980 in the form of *255DRY*, a former Leicester City Transport Leyland PD3A which had been acquired from Whippet Coaches.

This bus was painted into fleet livery but was sadly de-roofed at Cross Inn in November 1983. Two former Nottingham Daimler Fleetlines were also operated together with an ex-Newport Atlantean, *PDW99H*. Of the two Swifts, *516* lasted until 1986 when it became a source of spares for *518* which soldiered on until 1988. They are seen in John's yard at Llanharry on 20 July 1983. An ex-Merthyr Tydfil Leopard *EHB265G*, also bought from Brewers, was the only other saloon, but this was normally kept as a spare vehicle. All the buses were used for schools contracts, and after they were all sold on, K & P John carried on trading as a coach fleet until retiring in July 2002.

(John Wiltshire)